Your
NEXT
MOVE

YAHOO!® hotjobs®

Your
NEXT
MOVE

SUCCESS STRATEGIES FOR
MIDCAREER PROFESSIONALS

DAN FINNIGAN AND **MARC KARASU**

STERLING PUBLISHING
New York

Published by Sterling Publishing Co., Inc.
387 Park Avenue South, New York, NY 10016

Copyright © 2006 Yahoo! Inc. All rights reserved.

Distributed in Canada by Sterling Publishing
c/o Canadian Manda Group, 165 Dufferin Street
Toronto, Ontario M6K 3H6

Distributed in Great Britain by Chrysalis Books Group PLC
The Chrysalis Building, Bramley Road, London W10 6SP, England

Distributed in Australia by Capricorn Link (Australia) Pty. Ltd.
P.O. Box 704, Windsor, NSW 2756, Australia

Library of Congress Cataloging-in-Publication Data

Finnigan, Dan.
  Your next move : Yahoo! HotJobs success strategies for midcareer professionals /
Dan Finnigan and Marc Karasu.
    p. cm.
  ISBN 1-4027-2826-3
  1. Career changes—Computer network resources. 2.Job hunting—Computer network
resources. 3. Vocational guidance—Computer network resources. 4. World Wide Web.
5. Internet. I. Karasu, Marc. II. Title.

HF5384.F56 2006
650.14—dc22   2005026985

Printed in the United States of America

10 9 8 7 6 5 4 3 2 1

For information about custom editions, special sales, premium and corporate
purchases, please contact the Sterling Special Sales Department at 800-805-5489
or specialsales@sterlingpub.com

CONTENTS

Acknowledgments

Many wonderful, talented people helped us bring this book to fruition.
(It goes to show the power of a great network!) We'd like to thank
Laura Boswell, whose tireless work and dedication were essential to this book.
We're eternally grateful for the hard work and wisdom of Project Manager
Amy Werner, as well as that of our colleagues at Yahoo! HotJobs, including
Sean Bosker, Douglas Lee, Lauren Meller, Yahoo! Legal, Libby Sartain,
the Yahoo! Talent Acquisition team and our former colleagues Erin Hovanec,
Jason Gasdick, and Christopher Jones. We'd also like to thank the staff of
Barnes & Publishing, including our devoted editor, Meredith Peters Hale;
our publisher, Michael Fragnito, Production Manager Paulette Hodge; Creative
Director Jeffrey Batzli; Designer Wendy Ralphs; Managing Editor Maria Spano;
Pamela Wong; the agent for this series, John C. Leonhardt; and Stacey May
and Amy King for the book's elegant and efficient design. Many thanks to
the following for their input: Cheryl Ferguson, Patricia Shea, Harvey Laney,
Laura Donovan, Adam Dubois, Lisa Gravelle, Lynda Harrington, Will Houston,
Pat Katepoo, Sherry Miller, Kate Moody, Sean Perry, Jennifer Sander,
Jeff Sherman, Peter Weddle, Lou Adler, Matt Winkler and various staffers at
Society for Human Resources Management and the Bureau of Labor Statistics.
Last but not least, we'd like to thank our families and friends
for their support and inspiration.

Artist Credits for Chapter Openers

Chapter 1: Michael Maslin

Chapter 2: Lee Lorenz

Chapter 3: Robert Mankoff

Chapter 4: Mischa Richter

Chapter 5: Arnie Levin

Chapter 6: Charles Barsotti

Chapter 7: Harley L. Schwardron

Chapter 8: Jack Ziegler

Chapter 9: Warren Miller

Chapter 10: Leo Cullum

Introduction:
Onward. Upward.

Welcome back to the job hunt!

If you're reading this, chances are you have been out in the working world for some time and are now considering changing jobs—either because you'd like to or because you're being forced to by circumstances beyond your control. Believe it or not, no matter what the reason for your plunge into the job market, the prospect of finding new employment is something to be excited about!

After all, you can now focus on what you want, and find the job that best suits you. You're a "midcareer professional." You're no longer obliged to take whatever you can get. You have experience, a well-developed skill set, and a sincere desire to work hard and contribute to the success of an organization.

Yet you find yourself floundering. Maybe you've gotten off track from what you originally wanted to do. Maybe your "dream job" didn't turn out to be what you expected. Maybe you found a job you liked, but have been let go. Or maybe you simply hate your workplace.

Figuring out how to proceed is more complex now than when you were just starting out. You may have a spouse or family to consider; you might worry that mortgages and other commitments are preventing you from moving forward.

So how do you take that next big step in your career? Where do you begin?

THINK OPPORTUNITIES, NOT OBSTACLES

When confronted with changing a job or a career, many midcareer professionals immediately trot out all the reasons not to change—citing expenses, possible pay cuts, lack of proper training, and the challenges involved in starting over again at a new company. Essentially, they fear the unknown. For some job seekers, this fear is paralyzing.

Yet for others it is energizing. It can be that way for you, too.

Here's why you should welcome, rather than resist, exploring new career options: First, it is exciting to realize that, unlike workers of previous generations, you have unlimited companies and career fields to choose from. No longer are you tied to one job or one company for your entire life. As you grow and change, the work you do will change as well, and opportunities are out there to accommodate your developing professional needs.

No longer are career paths linear or seamless; you can move back and forth through many different kinds of jobs, if that's what it takes to ultimately realize your ambitions. You can take time off to explore other opportunities, or freelance and return to work again. Employers now place greater value on "soft" skills and life experience—you just have to find a way to demonstrate how your abilities and background can benefit them.

Second, you have technology to help you find, research, and land jobs. Online job boards can show you thousands of available positions anywhere in the world, and personal search agents can deliver them straight to your e-mail inbox. Company job sites can give you background information on the corporate culture and job expectations. In addition, the Internet can provide the latest news reports on growing (or declining) fields and companies.

Third, you have a valuable resource in the support of your network of family and friends. You don't have to do this alone. The people in your life can offer job leads, read over your resume, test your interviewing prowess, and give you feedback on jobs that are best for you.

HEALTHY, WEALTHY, AND WISE

Finally, think how much happier and healthier you'll be in a job you find rewarding and in a workplace that values your contributions. Draw on your past experiences and mistakes, and avoid applying for jobs that will sap your energy or keep you from your family and personal pursuits. You'll be more fulfilled—and, hopefully, more inspired to work hard and achieve success!

So join us as we explore the many advantages you possess as a midcareer professional, review some time-tested job-hunting strategies, and reveal tips and tricks you may not have considered before.

You have far more leverage than you may realize in today's job market, and more resources to help you than you'll even have time to use. There are many great jobs out there just waiting for you—let's go find the right one!

CHAPTER 1

Moving On:
How Do You Know
When It's Time to Go?

"Let's face it: you and this organization have never been a good fit."

Once in a while, one lucky person will select the right career path before the ink is even dry on his college diploma. Over the next five to ten years, his route will be as straight and smooth as a sword—he'll know exactly what he wants to do, learn the right skills, develop an impressive network, and shimmy up the corporate ladder with the ease of a monkey in a tree.

Yeah, we hate that guy too.

For the rest of the workforce, the first five to ten years aren't so much career *paths* as they are career *rivers*, with whitewater rapids of advancement, tributaries of school and family, and swamps of layoffs and self-doubt.

So you paddle your raft along for a few years, setting up camp every now and then at whatever job gives you shelter and a hot meal until you finally pitch your tent on the banks of your current job. It pays the mortgage, the benefits are pretty good, and it helps you support your family. Or if you're single, you can take a nice vacation each year, or maybe get that convertible you always wanted.

Still, as the days wear on, you find yourself deriving happiness from the benefits or the vacations or the car, but not your work. You want more direction, more purpose in your life than you have now, just grinding out forty hours (or more) a week to bring home a paycheck.

But you wonder what's around that next bend—a smooth, serene lake surrounded by emerald green meadows? Or a dangerous whirlpool? You're older now, have more responsibilities, and can't take the risks you used to when five roommates and dinners of ramen noodles were a perfectly satisfactory way of life.

However, the only way to find that new position—the one that sets your heart aflutter and gives your life meaning—is to set off on your raft once again and leave your current job behind. But is that the right decision now? And if so, how do you start? Or, if you're unemployed, how can you kickstart your career onto the right track this time?

In this chapter, we'll examine your reasons for seeking a new job and, if they're valid, give you tips on how to start looking for one that matches your needs—mentally, physically, and spiritually. We'll also offer you guidance on how to better plot the course for the rest of your career life.

THE SUNDAY SLUMP

You know the feeling—the sense of impending dread on Sunday nights, the flat feeling as you stare out the bus window on Monday morning, watching the clock as the day s-l-o-w-l-y inches toward five o'clock (or, more likely, six, seven, or eight o'clock).

You were so excited when you were offered this job, and early on you came to work each day with a spring in your step. But now you just want to crawl under your desk and take a nap until the workday's over. What went wrong with your job?

If you are unhappy in your job, take heart—a 2004 *BusinessWeek* survey of five hundred executives found that 72 percent were not in their "dream jobs." And a 2003 Conference Board survey showed that almost half of working Americans are unhappy with their jobs.

Why you are unhappy, however, goes to the heart of the matter. People cite a variety of personal and professional reasons for dissatisfaction at work, ranging from a long commute to a poor rapport with the boss to an inadequate salary. While there are some issues you can address easily, others may require a more drastic approach.

So how do you figure out which sources of dissatisfaction will respond to a quick fix and which ones will only be resolved by changing jobs? First, let's take a look at your current job and see what's causing your unhappiness. Then we'll evaluate whether you can fix the problem where you are.

Your Manager

Surveys have shown again and again that the number one reason people leave a job is not because of the salary or even the work itself—it's because of a bad relationship with their manager. Getting along with the boss is more important than pay or benefits when it comes to happiness at work, according to a 2003 survey by international staffing firm Accountemps, a division of Robert Half International, Inc. In the survey of one hundred fifty executives from large firms, 43 percent of respondents said employee–manager relationships have the greatest impact on job satisfaction.

"Employees are most productive when they feel their contributions are valued and their feedback is welcomed by management," said Max Messmer, chairman and CEO of Robert Half International, and author of *Motivating Employees for Dummies*. "The reverse is also true—an unsupportive atmosphere can lead to reduced performance levels and higher turnover for businesses."

Maybe your manager is overly demanding or unethical, or maybe your personalities just clash, but, bottom line, the manager-employee relationship will have a greater impact on your work happiness than anything else. If you can't find a way to get along with your boss, you may not be able to find happiness in your current work environment. Conversely, if you can improve this dynamic, the situation may be salvageable.

▶**Action Items:** Managing Expectations
Ask yourself how you feel about your manager:

- ☀ Is he unreasonably demanding (changing deadlines and expectations without warning, requiring you to work long hours/weekends, and so forth)?
- ☀ Does she give constructive feedback?
- ☀ Does he stand up for you when something goes wrong?
- ☀ Is she too much of a friend, and not enough of a leader?
- ☀ Do you respect your manager? If not, why not?

Answering questions like these will give you insight into whether you should meet with your manager to discuss your concerns, or if it's a lost cause.

You Don't Feel Valued or Your Contributions Go Unrecognized

Have you come up with creative solutions to problems only to see others get the credit? Do you have good ideas that seem to fall on deaf ears? Do you do 80 percent of the work but get only 20 percent of the credit? Does your manager know about all your accomplishments, yet still inserts the lackluster "Meets expectations" in your performance reviews? Employees want to feel that their work is important to their employers—those who don't will look elsewhere, and *should!*

Your Company Lacks Direction

One Hay Group survey found that only 27 percent of respondents said their organizations have a clear sense of where they are going. People need and want solid leadership, and they need to know that their company has realistic, exciting goals. A company that keeps changing course will lose employees.

Loss of Trust in Your Company or Its Leadership

As the Internet Age surged in the '90s, dot-com companies appeared overnight—then disappeared just as quickly. The stock market reached record highs, yet thousands of employees who worked eighty-hour weeks for stock options never saw a dime. Corporate executives in scandal-ridden companies like Enron, WorldCom, and Tyco left employees with little money and much distrust in their leadership.

Whether a company is struggling because of poor decisions or outright deception, employees don't want to be a part of it. In today's real-time culture, word travels fast when a company is floundering—and employees jump ship.

No Growth Opportunities

You could very well love your job, and be great at it, but when you think one, five, or ten years down the road, you don't see yourself fitting in there. For example, maybe the next step up for you at your current company is management, but you prefer being "in the trenches" rather than overseeing other people's performance. Or perhaps the next job you were hoping for was just filled by someone else and you don't know when another one like it will open up again.

Ask yourself: How far do I want to go in this company? In this field? Is there training or another initiative I could take to create a better opportunity for myself here? Consider whether the problem lies in your own inertia, or if you have truly hit a dead end.

Not Enough Challenge

You've become so adept at your job that you're simply bored. You want a position that will help you grow each day and provide you with the skills and training that will propel you to the next level.

Take Kathleen, for example, a Chicago-area insurance sales rep who loved her industry but found that her job had become too routine. She left to become a consultant at an insurance/risk management consulting firm, and found a much better fit. She got to remain in her industry, even working with some of the same contacts, but with a greater emphasis on finding solutions instead of selling. You may be able to add new responsibilities to your current position. Or, like Kathleen, to achieve the growth you desire, you may need to make a move.

Disappointment with Your Job or Field

Now that you've been in the working world for several years, you're beginning to know what you do and don't want. Your current job is simply not what you expected. Maybe you thought you'd enjoy constant travel, but find it exhausting. Or perhaps you've discovered that you are much more introverted than you thought, and making big presentations isn't for you. It's not your fault—but it is time to move on.

Work Environment

Much like your manager, your work environment—culture, coworkers, hours, commute, noise level, and so forth—figures in how you view your job as well. Throw in one too many gossipy coworkers or delayed trains and you may find the frustration outweighing the pluses of the job.

Lack of Meaning

At some point, everyone asks the question: "What should I do with my life?"
Some people are content to work at their job eight hours a day, then do volunteer
work for a cause they support in their spare time. For others that is not enough—
they want their work itself to make a difference in the world.

For example, Stephen had earned his law degree but didn't want to work at a
law firm. Instead, he took a job with a nonprofit, helping at-risk kids stay in school.
His public defender experience made it easy for him to navigate the justice system, helping his clients stay on the right track; meanwhile, seeing the immediate
impact of his work in kids' lives was worth far more than a big paycheck.

You Want to Be Your Own Boss

Now this one is tricky. All of us dream at some point of working for ourselves, but
starting your own business is a complicated and risky venture. While deciding
whether to go the self-employment route is beyond the scope of this book, consider these questions as you contemplate launching a business of your own:

☼ Can I work alone or do I need the stimulation of an office environment?

☼ Do I have the experience and /or portfolio to offer a great service?

☼ Can I support myself financially while I'm getting established?

☼ Am I comfortable with risk and uncertainty?

☼ Do I really want to work from home, or just *be* home?

Work-Life Balance

Despite our many gadgets and labor-saving devices, Americans are still stressed
out and work more hours than many of the world's workers.

Economist Juliet Schor, in her 1993 bestseller *The Overworked American:
The Unexpected Decline of Leisure*, argued that the United States "is the world's
standout workaholic nation." By the end of 2004, a Harris Interactive poll found
that nearly two-thirds of workers saw their workloads increasing, with more than
10 percent of respondents working an extra ten hours a week or more. More
than half answered "No" when asked, "Do you feel your employer appreciates
and rewards you well?"

And even though more companies are offering perks like flex-time, child care,
and concierge services, still, a 2004 survey by travel Web site Expedia.com
found that Americans failed to use an estimated 415 million vacation days that
year—an average of three days per worker!

Employees need to be able to balance their work and personal lives for the sake of their health and that of their families. Even at a family-friendly company, a job that demands long hours with little time to relax, exercise, eat right, or spend time with family and friends will eventually wear you down.

hot facts

Not Just a Job

A 2003 survey by research and consulting firm Yankelovich found that more than half (55%) of working respondents think of their employment as a career and not a job—therefore, you want it to be more than just punching in and out every day.

Money

You didn't think we'd forget this one, did you? Of course, salary and benefits are important to workers, and those who don't get what they feel they deserve will eventually harbor resentment and leave.

If you are one of these people, before you go, consider:

- ☼ *Asking for a raise:* Meet with your supervisor and present evidence of your accomplishments and worth to the bottom line. Use the Yahoo! HotJobs salary tool to research ahead of time what others in your position in your geographic region are making.
- ☼ *Asking for more perks:* Tuition assistance, parking, flex-time—benefits like these are negotiable and can be as valuable or even more valuable than cold hard cash.

▶Action Items: Five for the Road?
List the top five reasons you want to leave your current job.

1. _____
2. _____
3. _____
4. _____
5. _____

Now, evaluate whether these are issues that can be addressed by talking with your manager and negotiating a better situation—or if they are telltale signs that it's time to leave.

For example, are you working weekends frequently because of a short-term project that will soon end, or because your manager needs you to make up for her mistakes? Have you been passed over for a promotion because you aren't yet up to the responsibilities (but in time will be)—or do you believe that you are more than ready, but someone with less experience but more pull was given the job? Situations that can be improved with more time and work on your part might be worth the effort, especially if you like the company. But if you are already doing the best you can and don't see any chance for improvement in sight, then making a change may be a wise decision.

 **THINK Outside the Box**

The More Things Change...

Sometimes you don't have to change companies to change jobs. Amy had worked in sales for a major computer corporation for nearly twenty years when the demanding quotas and constant travel started taking their toll. After various aches and pains and a bout with depression, she decided she needed a change. However, with twenty years invested she didn't want to give up her great benefits and accumulated vacation time. Instead, she moved into a marketing position in the same company. While Amy took a pay cut and no longer receives commissions, she is happy to be doing something different—and keeping the rewards she has stored up over the years.

ASSESS YOURSELF

Now that you've highlighted the unhappy aspects of your job, you may be ready to leave skid marks by your desk.

Don't hand in your resignation letter just yet—you don't want to jump from the frying pan into the fire! Before you seek out a new opportunity, you need to assess yourself and your life situation, to ensure that your next job aligns with your personal needs and skills.

The good news is that at this point in your life, you have enough experience and know yourself well enough to make a much more targeted choice than you did when you were first entering the workforce. You may find that you are in the wrong career altogether. While making a complete career change is a subject for another book, we will include that possibility in the next sections for you to consider. As you read on and complete the activities, think about what kind of work will meet your needs, and then figure out whether it's a job change or a complete career change that you should be contemplating.

Hard and Soft Skills

You're probably familiar with *hard* and *soft* skills. Now that you've had a few jobs, chances are you've gained more of these skills than you realize. Some of these skills you'll want to strengthen, others you'll want to leave behind, and still others you'll want and need to develop to help you advance in your career. So here's a quick refresher.

Hard skills are the measurable abilities and/or certifications you have acquired from practice, schooling, or training: Foreign language skills, Adobe Illustrator, computer networking, Bachelor of Science, and so on. Depending on your career path to this point, you may be highly skilled in a few similar areas or have broader experience; either way, it's time to decide which of these skills you want and need to continue strengthening in future jobs, and which you can do without.

▶**Action Items: Hard (Skills) of the Matter**
Write down five (or more, if you prefer) of your hard skills, focusing on those you use most on a day-to-day basis in your current job. As you make your list, consider which skills you most enjoy using, and which you don't (if any) and why.

1. _____

2. _____

3. _____

4. _____

5. _____

Now that you've identified some of your hard skills, ask yourself the following questions:

☀ Do you want to continue using these skills in your career? Just because you are good at something doesn't mean that's what you enjoy doing as a job. For example, you may have gained a great deal of financial experience as a loan officer, but find that it's not studying facts and figures you like as much as helping people plan their finances to achieve their dreams.

☼ Do you have other hard skills that you're not tapping in your current position? Think about other jobs for which you're qualified. For guidance, use the *Occupational Outlook Handbook* (OOH) to find jobs where your skills are needed. (See page 77 to learn more about the OOH.)

By contrast, *soft skills* are those intangible qualities that outfit you for some jobs and fields better than others—think communication skills, team building and motivation, listening, compassion, and so forth.

Have you ever been told that you're a great communicator, or that you have a way with kids? While certain soft skills can be learned, most tend to be talents for which you have a natural aptitude. Soft skills are the secret to finding work that is better suited to you, even if right now you lack the practical experience. Some experts have even argued that these skills matter more than intelligence or technical skills when it comes to succeeding on the job!

▶Action Items: Finding Your Softer Side

Write down five soft skills you have—tendencies you were born with or skills you've gained from your profession, your volunteer work, and your general life experience. Take into account all the positions you've held, not just your current job:

1. _____

2. _____

3. _____

4. _____

5. _____

Be aware, as you categorize your soft skills, that (as with hard skills) you may possess certain abilities that you don't care to use in the future. Going forward, you'll want to consider jobs that draw on the skills you have and the ones you like to use.

From the Desk of

Max Messmer
Chairman and CEO, Robert Half International, Inc.

A generation ago, career planning was relatively simple. You chose a particular field or industry and spent most, if not all, of your career there—often with a single employer. In fact, twenty-five years ago if you asked employees where they saw themselves in five years, many would have said with the same company but in a more senior role.

Ask that question of the average person today and the answer may surprise you. Many people have no idea what direction they want their careers to take. If they do, they often lack a clear strategy for getting there.

In my role as CEO of a specialized staffing firm, I work with professionals at all stages of their careers. Many are contemplating their next move but are unsure where to begin. My advice is always to start by developing a plan. Carefully assess what you do best and what you enjoy doing. With any luck, the two coincide.

Consider how you might respond to the following questions: In five years, what do you want to be doing each day, and under what conditions? Do you see yourself employed with a large or small firm? Are you working independently or as part of a team? Is achieving a better work/life balance a major goal? Is money your chief motivator or is it more important to support a cause that is meaningful to you?

Write down your answers to these questions and list any other ambitions you may have. These may change over time, but committing them to writing will help you create short- and long-term objectives that are achievable. For each goal, assign specific action items—and give yourself deadlines for completing them.

Just as our personal lives change, so do our professional lives. Consider your career a work in progress. As you accomplish each goal, add new ones. Having a plan will provide you with an objective and a sense of purpose—both of which are pivotal in achieving long-term professional growth and satisfaction.

RHI is the world's first and largest specialized staffing firm.

Personality

Some people work well under pressure and others don't. Some people don't get going until midday; others are "morning people." These are just a couple of examples of how personality figures into your work.

Your personality is the sum of the distinctive inner qualities that make up who you are as a person. Now that you've been in the working world for a while, you've discovered that certain personality traits—good or bad—are probably here to stay and should be weighed as you look for your next job.

For example, if you're outgoing and a good communicator, maybe technical writing isn't for you—but writing marketing copy is. Similarly, if you aren't a detail-oriented person, you might not be cut out for forensics.

▶ **Action Items: The Unique You**

Write down five of your personality traits (think "outgoing," "energetic," "sensitive," and so forth):

1. _____

2. _____

3. _____

4. _____

5. _____

Now ask yourself: Do these traits fit into the culture at your current company? Into the career you've chosen as a whole? If not, think of jobs where these characteristics might be valued assets.

Interests

While knitting, restoring furniture, or making your world-famous taco pie might not be talents you'd want to list on your resume, your interests can say a lot about you. They might be the very things you would want to do with your life if money were not a factor.

Examining your interests can give you insight into job options you might not have considered before. For example, if you enjoy travel, you might look into working as a travel agent or taking a job at a PR agency that promotes cruise lines. If you're a lawyer tired of waiting to become partner, perhaps you could apply your skills to a nonprofit whose cause you'd like to champion.

▶**Action Items: What Interests You?**

To get a better idea of your interests, ask yourself these questions:

    ☼ What was I doing the last time I completely lost track of time?

    ☼ If I could do anything I wanted and be paid for it, what would it be?

    ☼ My ideal weekend is spent doing _____.

Think about whether you can pursue these interests in your current job. If not, consider what other jobs or careers might give you a chance to do so.

Work Quirks

Work quirks are those little things you need to do your best work. When you picture yourself in your next job, what do you see? Do you like having your coworkers as friends, or do you prefer to keep your work and social life separate? Do you like a structured workday or more freedom to make your own schedule? Do you like team projects or working more independently? Think about your ideal work environment and then try to find companies that put a premium on that kind of work setting. Not that you should only accept jobs from companies that have gourmet coffee in the break rooms. You likely won't be able to satisfy your every need. But you do want to try to find a workplace whose culture allows you to feel comfortable and be productive.

▶**Action Items: Quirks That Work**

Write down five of your "work quirks." Consider whether these factors are present or missing from your current job. Which ones would you need to make you happy at a new job?

1. _____

2. _____

3. _____

4. _____

5. _____

Values

We spend a third of our lives at work, so you want your company and your job to reflect—or at least not directly conflict with—your personal beliefs. If your company's priorities violate your beliefs relating to issues like politics, religion, or the environment, you won't be happy working there.

Luckily, it's easy to research companies' reputations on the Web, as well as positive initiatives they take, such as "days of service" working in the community.

▶**Action Items: Putting Values into Action**
List the five values you desire most in a workplace (qualities such as "honesty," "environmental responsibility," or "giving back to the community"):

1. _____

2. _____

3. _____

4. _____

5. _____

Consider whether the companies you've worked for so far have supported your values, and look for companies in the future that share those values.

CHANGING CAREERS

As you've reviewed why you want to leave your current job, you may have uncovered a larger truth: The problem may lie not in the job, but rather in your chosen field. The following resources may help you decide on your next move.

Assessment Tests

You've probably taken these before—tests like the Myers-Briggs or the Keirsey Temperament Sorter. But maybe it's time to try them again, to gain some new insights into how your personality has developed in the last few years.

A variety of exercises and tests are useful in helping you understand your personality and inner qualities. You can take them online, or through employment agencies, career counseling firms, your local adult education center, or libraries.

If cost is prohibitive, there are also Web sites and books with these tests (we list a few at the end of this chapter). You won't get a professional's interpretation, but they can give you an idea of where you stand.

Career Counselors

We'll go into more detail about career coaches and counselors in chapter 3. But if you find a reputable one and you do have the means, a career counselor can be very helpful in guiding you to your next career step.

▶Action Items: It's Never Too Late

One big hurdle many midcareer job seekers face is concern over how far they think they've gotten off their career track. They worry that time is passing them by, and they've missed their chance to do the great things they had planned to accomplish when they were young.

Well, true, it may be too late for you to become an astronaut, a ballerina, *and* a fireman, but there's no reason to abandon all your dreams either!

So take a moment and write down the jobs or activities that interested you when you were a child.

1. _____

2. _____

3. _____

4. _____

5. _____

What captivated you about these jobs? The excitement? Fame and fortune? Or were you interested simply because you were good at what it took to excel in these fields (acting, math, running)? Are there any "real-world" jobs that incorporate elements of these things you loved before the world got in the way of your dreams?

TO CHANGE JOBS OR NOT TO CHANGE JOBS: THAT IS THE QUESTION

Changing jobs is a big step, and one that can have a ripple effect through your life and the lives of others now that you're a more experienced worker. We hope this chapter has helped you at least begin the process of searching for a better job for yourself—or realize that you may be better off where you are for now.

But if you're ready to go, take a look at the next chapter to begin preparing for the obstacles you may face as you start your job search.

Recommended Books

I Don't Know What I Want, But I Know It's Not This: A Step-by-Step Guide to Finding Gratifying Work by Julie Jansen (Penguin Group, 2003, ISBN 0142002488, $14.00).

The Overworked American: The Unexpected Decline of Leisure by Juliet B. Schor (Basic Books, 1993, ISBN 046505434X, $16.50).

Emotional Intelligence by Daniel Goleman (Bantam Books, 1997, ISBN 0553375067, $17.00).

Working With Emotional Intelligence by Daniel Goleman (Bantam Books, 2000, ISBN 0553378589, $17.00)

What Should I Do with My Life? The True Story of People Who Answered the Ultimate Question by Po Bronson (Random House, Inc., 2003, ISBN 0375758984, $14.95).

Do What You Are: Discover the Perfect Career for You through the Secrets of Personality Type by Paul D. Tieger & Barbara Barron-Tieger, Deborah Baker, Editor (Little, Brown & Company, 2001, ISBN 0316880655, $18.95).

Discover What You're Best At: A Complete Career System That Lets You Test Yourself to Discover Your Own True Career Abilities by Linda Gale (Simon & Schuster, 1998, ISBN 0684839563, $14.00).

Please Understand Me II: Temperament, Character, Intelligence by David W. Keirsey (Prometheus Nemesis Book Company, Inc., 1998, ISBN 1885705026, $15.95).

Recommended Web Sites

Yahoo! HotJobs—Assessments:
http://hotjobs.yahoo.com/assessment

Yahoo! Salary Tool:
http://hotjobs.yahoo.com/salary

Assessment.com—Assessment and appraisals:
www.assessment.com

Humanmetrics—Jung Typology Test (Provides your personality formula, preferences, and a description of your type):
www.humanmetrics.com/cgi-win/JTypes1.htm

The Temperament Sorter II (registration required):
www.advisorteam.com/temperament_sorter

Queendom—Career Tests:
www.queendom.com

Hoovers.com—Research site for companies, industries, and leaders:
www.hoovers.com

Business Wire—Latest news on industries and companies:
www.businesswire.com

2

Consider This:
Thinking Through the
Challenges to Change

"First of all, Harrington, let me tell you how much we all admire your determination not to choose between job and family."

Remember that feeling when you began your first job search? You were scared, sure, but excited too. The entire world was open to you—you could move anywhere, apply for any kind of job, and you only had yourself to worry about.

But now that a few years (and a few jobs) have been added to your resume, you probably have more to consider as you ponder a job change. For example, it may not simply be "your" job change anymore—you might have a spouse and children to take into account now. And if you're single, mortgages or rents, benefits, and geographic location are just a few of the other realities that can factor into your decision—not to mention managing a job search while working at your current job.

In the first chapter we looked at reasons to consider changing your job. Now we're going to evaluate the challenges in making a job change—how to manage them successfully, and even how to use them as opportunities to bring you closer to the career you've always wanted.

It's a Family Affair

Married, in a relationship, or single, it doesn't matter—you need to involve your loved ones as you look for another job. Not only are their feelings about your job change important, but they can serve as sounding boards and offer you much-needed support.

Obviously, if you have a significant other, you'll need to get his input—especially if a new job will require a pay cut or relocation. He may have his own job and career path he wants and deserves to pursue. In addition, if your taking a new job will mean your significant other will have to support you both for a time, you'll need to discuss that with him and begin to formulate a revised spending plan for that period.

There are many issues to address with a partner when considering a job change. Here are just a few of them:

- ☼ How would a job change affect your time at home? Would the new job mean a longer commute, longer hours away from home, and so forth?

- ☼ How would a job change affect your relationship? For example, if you have to relocate for a new job, will your significant other come along, or would you attempt a long-distance relationship?

- ☼ Have you recently started or hope soon to start a family? You may want to postpone a major job change if you have a baby on the way.

- ☼ According to the American Association of Retired Persons (AARP), in 2005 more than 30 million Americans were caring for an ailing parent, relative, or friend. If you face this situation, it could affect whether you should change jobs—especially if your current work situation has a generous family leave policy.

- ☼ Are you both in good health? If either of you (or a child) is having health concerns, you'll want to consider your combined benefits and sick time, and whether your new job will give you the flexibility to address those concerns. (See pages 34–35 for more on benefits to consider before leaving your current job.)

- ☼ Are you planning a vacation? How much vacation time do you both currently have coming? (You may want to take that Disney vacation your kids have been begging for while you still have paid time off.)

- ☼ Would your significant other be happy in another city? If not, can you forge a compromise?

Of course, your significant other may welcome the change—she loves you and wants you to be happy, after all. Her enthusiasm can add another level of support as you're embarking on your job search—through helping to send out resumes, proofread cover letters, and practice interviewing techniques, as well as reminding you of skills you've overlooked.

Meanwhile, if you have children, their welfare is another huge consideration as you weigh the pros and cons of your job change. For example:

- ☼ How would a pay cut or period with only one income affect your children's activities or schooling?

- ☼ Will your children be able to adapt easily to a new city, a new school, and new friends?

- ☼ Would a new job require you to spend more time traveling, and less time at Little League games?

- ☼ Are your children performing well or struggling in school?

Remember, too, that your kids can be an inspiration to you as you're looking for a better position—one that not only provides better for them financially, but provides them with a happier parent as well.

Single people also need to consider their families as they change jobs, even if those "families" simply comprise a circle of parents, siblings, pets, and friends. Parents and siblings can offer advice based on their own life experience and how well they know your personality. And friends can be a much-needed support system as well as a network to help you find a new job. So regardless of your marital situation, your loved ones can be a valuable resource as you consider your next career move. Involve them early and often, and you'll make the right choice.

take a memo

Dina's Story

Dina never wanted to be a stay-at-home mom—she loved working in her chosen field of human resources. But as her Army officer husband was transferred from one city to another, she chose to remain home with the kids.

After seven years of constant moving, Dina got a call from a large nonprofit with an offer to work in the organization's benefits department. But there was one problem: Her husband had just been transferred to England. Together, they agreed that she should take the job, and the younger of their two sons, back to the United States during her husband's year overseas.

The transition was difficult for Dina, despite the strong support she got from her husband. People openly questioned her commitment to her family. But she knew she was doing the right thing—her older son was happy in his school abroad and would have wonderful memories of his time there. Meanwhile, she and her younger son could finally establish a household in the States, instead of moving from apartment to apartment, and her husband could come back and retire while she had the job of her dreams. The short-term compromises were difficult, but in the end they led to happiness for the whole family.

FINANCIALLY FLUMMOXED?

Here's the first question that runs through your mind as you seriously begin a job search: *Can I afford to change jobs?*

It's easy—and understandable—to worry about money as you're contemplating a job change. Worries like the following abound:

- ☼ I can't take a pay cut until I finish paying off my school loans.
- ☼ We just bought a house—I need to stay at my job to pay the mortgage.
- ☼ If I leave my job, we won't have on-site child care anymore.

If you are interviewing for jobs that pay more than you currently make, coping with the financial aspects of a job change won't be a challenge. But if you are unemployed, will be unemployed soon, or are looking into jobs that will mean a large pay cut, you'll need to give your finances some honest consideration.

First and foremost, you should try to stay in your current job until you find another one and therefore avoid any gaps in pay. Certainly there are times and situations that will necessitate leaving a job without having another one lined up, but if at all possible, keep your current job and let your search energize you and keep you thinking about tomorrow (while your paychecks are still coming in today).

If you are unemployed, you may want to consider applying for unemployment benefits or taking a part-time job or freelance work while you conduct your job search. This will not only be a boost financially, but may help you make contacts that lead to future jobs.

Meanwhile, even if you are doing very well financially, it's always wise to take a good look at your income and expenses—this will help your money go further no matter how much you make. Tracking your expenses can help you do away with unnecessary spending. Or, you might find that you have a greater cushion than you thought, and, by monitoring your spending carefully, you could afford to take a more rewarding job with a lower salary.

▶**Action Item: Money Matters**

Sit down with your receipts, bank statements, and a notebook and ask yourself the following questions:

- ☼ How much money do you have in your checking and savings accounts? If you have to leave your current job, do you have enough savings to live on while you search for a job?

- ☼ How much will your new job pay? (Use Yahoo! HotJobs' salary tool and the Department of Labor's *Occupational Outlook Handbook* for research.)

- ☼ What are the major payments you need to make each month (rent, mortgage, car loan, and so forth)?

- ☼ Does your spouse make enough to support you both during your job search?

- ☼ Do you keep track of your spending or do you just "wing it"?

 **THINK Outside the Box**

Unemployed Doesn't Mean Unwanted

You can find solid sources of income while you are unemployed—you just have to be willing to look for them.

Part-time work: Part-time jobs today involve more than sweeping floors or pumping gas, and people of all ages are taking them. They can provide a lot more than minimum wage, too; some offer health insurance and 401(k) plans for eligible employees. Part-time work gives you structure and gets you out of the house—putting you in contact with other people who can offer you full-time jobs!

Friends, family, and neighbors: Many people feel more comfortable paying someone they know to baby-sit, clean house, tutor a child, repair a computer, or walk their dog than they do hiring a stranger. If someone you know needs services like these, offer to do them for a fee (if you feel comfortable doing so). If you are good at landscaping, car detailing, or the like, friends and neighbors might truly appreciate your initiative.

Speak up: Do you have a special skill you can teach others? Is there a subject you can write or speak about in your community? Investigate how you can make the most of your knowledge and skills, whether or not they are related to your career. Many community centers, churches, and adult education programs offer seminars taught by regular folks just like you. You'd be surprised how many people will pay to learn something you know.

Unemployment pay: If you have been laid off, you may qualify for unemployment insurance payments. While unemployment insurance won't totally replace your lost earnings (and you will have to pay deferred taxes on them at tax time), it can help you make ends meet as you're looking for another job. To apply, first contact your previous employer's HR department to see if you qualify. Then work with your state's employment commission (you can find it at http://www.dol.gov) to submit the proper paperwork and claim forms to begin receiving your checks. Local offices may offer resources such as counseling, Internet access, resume writing, and job leads.

☼ How high is your credit card debt? Investigate ways to lower your debt—transferring the balances to a home equity line of credit, for example.

☼ Which everyday expenses can you cut out to save money? Magazines? Unused gym memberships? Cable TV? Take-out food? Lattes? Little luxuries like these can add up quickly.

It's important to remember at this point in your life that you're not just living for today. You need to consider your future and that of your family, if you have one—retirement income, kids' college tuition, and other necessities.

However, you also have to remember that you're not making this change for money alone, but to derive more satisfaction from your career. With proper planning and advice, you can get past the money hurdle. Yes, you and your family need food and shelter, but beyond the necessities of life, how you spend your money is a matter of choice. You can choose to cut back for a few months if it means finding a job that gives your life meaning.

For example, Kelly, a copyeditor bored with her current job, decided to find something more fulfilling. She loved kids and wanted to make a career working with them. However, she had recently become engaged and had a wedding to plan. She discussed her hopes with her fiancé, who supported her completely. She left her job and began working as a preschool teacher. Professionally, she was still using her communication skills, but in a completely different environment, and becoming, in her words, "poor as I've ever been, but so happy."

BALANCING A JOB AND A JOB SEARCH

Looking for a job on the sly? Chances are you're not alone. Your coworkers are probably doing the same thing right now. If they're smart, you'll never be able to guess which ones. You need to be just as careful!

hot facts •

In a recent poll, Yahoo! HotJobs found that 47 percent of workers are currently looking for another job or plan to start a job search within the next twelve months.

Because a job search can be a job in itself, balancing your search while holding down a job—keeping it private, managing your time, not to mention balancing family and other priorities—is a major undertaking. But it's one well worth taking on! Why? Because although you may have to give up some lunch breaks and weekends to craft your resume or go on interviews, it's well worth it to find a better job.

Here are some points to consider as you search for employment—while you're employed.

Make a Schedule

Have you ever noticed that you tend to work harder and be better organized when you have a lot to do? As you begin looking for a new job, set aside definite blocks of time for your job search each week. Let your family and friends know you need certain evenings and weekends to work on your job search, and promise yourself you will not take on any activities during those times—even volunteer work. Hire a sitter, a dog walker, or a housekeeper if you have to. If you start setting boundaries now for yourself and those around you, you'll maintain your sanity and get more done.

 THINK Outside the Box

When "Distractions" Are Your Life

Avoiding distractions is often easier said than done. If you're a parent or have other major responsibilities, you can't always put them on hold to look for a job. If you're unemployed, you may be working part time or trying to drum up freelance work. All this takes time and energy.

What you need to do is carve out time for your search. Make a plan that details when you're going to work on your job search and for how long. Specify dates and times. Then set some goals, no matter how limited, for that time.

For example, plan to spend one hour every other day on your job search. Then devote certain days to searching online for jobs and other days to sending out resumes. You'll make progress one step at a time.

Keep Your Current Job

We've said it before and we'll say it again: If at all possible, keep your current job while you search for another one. If you're currently employed, it's best to remain employed if you can. Don't believe those stories you hear about the guys who cash in their 401(k)s, move to the Caribbean, and open a dive shop. Sure, it does happen, but for now, be realistic and focus on the jobs within your reach. (And don't you dare cash in your 401[k]!)

Perform Well at Work

Once you get started with your job search, you may find that your current job seems even more tedious than before. And once you get a good lead on a job, you may feel like ignoring your current job altogether. Don't let this happen!

Continue to do your best at your current job. If you eventually leave, you want it to be on your terms—not because your manager noticed a downturn in your work and had cause to let you go.

One worker, Matt, did not heed this advice. He had decided to quit his Web-writing job to go back to school full time, but the next semester didn't start for another three months. Rather than making the most of his work time, he kept his plans to himself and began taking days off and calling in sick to use up his paid time off. Finally his manager sat him down to ask what was going on, and Matt had to fess up—two months before he had planned to leave. He got to keep his job but left on bad terms with his manager and coworkers. It might not have directly affected his career right then, but he lost any chance of getting good references or contacts from that job for the future.

Another tip is to avoid searching during business hours—it's too easy to get caught by a manager passing by your monitor. If you need time for a job interview, use vacation or personal time. Don't call in sick.

Maintain Your Privacy

Keeping your job search a secret from your current employer is paramount, so be wary of the following:

- ☼ **Computers.** Many companies monitor employee computer use, so use your home computer or one at a library, copy shop, or Internet café for your job search. And don't use your work e-mail address—create one in Yahoo! solely for job searching. Avoid the office fax machine, printer, and photocopier too—it's easy to leave a copy of your resume or cover letter in one of them. Again, use a home office, local library, or copy shop.

- ☼ **Phones.** Don't use your work phone for calls related to your job search—especially long distance calls. Use a cell phone or schedule a time when you can call from home without interruptions. Using company property to conduct your job search is convenient, but it's also risky.

- ☼ **Coworkers.** Never tell coworkers you're looking for a new job. Even the most trusted confidantes can inadvertently blow your cover.

- ☼ **Resumes.** Your company may use the same job boards you do to find employees. Don't let your resume pop up when they do! Use a tool like Yahoo! HotJobs' HotBlock. (More on this feature in chapter 5.) This exclusive tool may allow you to control who sees your resume, and who doesn't. List your home address and phone number (or cell phone number) on your resume. Don't include your business contact information.

☼ **Attire.** Dress for success, but be discreet. Unless you wear one every day, don't show up at your current job sporting a fancy suit. Bring a change of clothing or conceal your jacket or tie (for men) in a bag. Try to avoid going on interviews during business hours; instead, schedule interviews before or after work or over lunch. You can also schedule multiple interviews on one day and then take personal or vacation time.

THE RELOCATION SITUATION

Location, location, location. As the real estate agents say, it can go a long way in determining your happiness.

A change of geography can be enormously energizing. Still, there are risks in moving. Your new company may not pay any relocation costs. You might make a higher salary by moving to New York, but the cost of living could wipe out any increase in pay. Large, affordable homes in the Southeast might tempt you, but if your sister back home in Boise can't help out with the baby-sitting, the big house won't do you much good.

Then of course there are the headaches of packing, moving, finding new doctors, changing your children's schools—you're not just moving jobs, you're moving entire lives. How do you know it's worth it? Does it really rain a lot in Seattle? Is Chicago actually that windy? Is the housing market that tough in southern California?

First, you need to decide whether to stay where you are. Are you happy where you live? Have you put down deep roots in your community? Are you near family and friends? Is your commute tolerable? In five years will there still be opportunities where you live? What do you like most and least about your community—and do the pros outweigh the cons?

Consider, too, the things that inspire you away from work. If kayaking and mountain climbing are your passions, then maybe Denver is the right place to move. Like the noise and action of a big city? Be sure your chosen destination is within reach of the culture and excitement that stimulates you.

▶**Action Items: Relocation Considerations**
Consider the following items as they apply to your current location. Now, next to each category, check off whether it is a positive ("Pro") or a negative ("Con") in your life right now. For example, if the cost of housing where you're living is too high, mark it as a "Con." If the crime rate is low, check "Pro." If job

opportunities in your field or at your experience level are limited, check "Con." Total up your pros and cons, and see what, if any, negatives can be turned into positives where you are—for example, carpooling to save money on your commute. If the cons still outweigh the pros, a job elsewhere might be the best choice for you.

	Pro	Con
Cost of Housing	☐	☐
Cost of Living	☐	☐
City/State Taxes on Earnings	☐	☐
Weather/Climate	☐	☐
Commute	☐	☐
Schools/Child Care	☐	☐
Crime Rate	☐	☐
Neighbors	☐	☐
Friends/Family	☐	☐
Activities	☐	☐
House of Worship	☐	☐
Health Care	☐	☐
Roots/Community Involvement	☐	☐
Job Options	☐	☐

If you are happy where you are, then relocation is probably not a good choice for you at this point. Check local job listings and tap into your network for jobs in your geographic area.

However, as much as you love Anytown, you may find there are no advertising jobs there or that the accounting firms there aren't hiring applicants at your level. Or you may just be ready for a change of scenery. In that case, you'll want to search for jobs in other areas.

Luckily, the Internet is a great resource for long-distance job searching. For example, on Yahoo! HotJobs, not only can you search a city (Philadelphia) but the surrounding metro area (Wilmington, Atlantic City) as well.

Additionally, the Yahoo! HotJobs salary tool helps you see what your job pays in other regions, while message boards allow you to "talk" with other job seekers in the regions that interest you and get a feel for where you're considering moving.

For the purposes of this book, we're focusing on the job, not the geography. To find a fulfilling career, you should *go where the jobs are*—even if it's your own backyard. Choose your destination with research and without regret, knowing that wherever you go you will make friends, have fun, and learn more skills to advance your career.

hot facts

Cities with the Most Jobs Posted on Yahoo! HotJobs:

1. New York, NY	18. Philadelphia, PA	35. Toronto, ONT
2. Chicago, IL	19. Indianapolis, IN	36. Richmond, VA
3. San Francisco, CA	20. Phoenix, AZ	37. Tucson, AZ
4. Denver, CO	21. Irvine, CA	38. Columbus, OH
5. San Jose, CA	22. Miami, FL	39. Pittsburgh, PA
6. Los Angeles, CA	23. Seattle, WA	40. Fremont, CA
7. San Diego, CA	24. Santa Clara, CA	41. Las Vegas, NV
8. Atlanta, GA	25. Tampa, FL	42. McLean, VA
9. Boston, MA	26. Pasadena, CA	43. Portland, OR
10. Salt Lake City, UT	27. Austin, TX	44. Jacksonville, FL
11. Dallas, TX	28. Minneapolis, MN	45. Scottsdale, AZ
12. Washington, DC	29. Baltimore, MD	46. Walnut Creek, CA
13. Sunnyvale, CA	30. Orlando, FL	47. Cleveland, OH
14. Houston, TX	31. Mountain View, CA	48. Milwaukee, WI
15. Sacramento, CA	32. Charlotte, NC	49. Hartford, CT
16. Oakland, CA	33. El Segundo, CA	50. Plano, TX
17. Cincinnati, OH	34. Detroit, MI	

NO MORE PENCILS, NO MORE BOOKS?

When you graduated from college, you probably thought you'd never have to enter the hallowed halls of an educational institution again.

But now that you are further along in your career, maybe you've found you have plateaued and need to improve your knowledge and skills. Or you may find that the promotions or jobs you are seeking require a graduate degree, or a level of technical expertise you have not acquired on the job. It's time to go back to school.

But how? You may be saying to yourself:

- ☼ I'm already working—where will I find the time?
- ☼ I have to get out of this job ASAP—I don't have two years to get another degree!
- ☼ I barely scrape by now. How can I afford to go back to school?

Good news! There are many paths today for working professionals to get the education they need to advance, without causing major upheaval in their lives—or breaking their bank accounts.

What Kind of Education Do You Need?

First of all, you may not need an entirely new degree to get a better job. Maybe you need a certificate in the latest computer scripting method, or to learn Spanish for business with Latin American clients. Luckily, today many companies offer classes in these types of skills on-site. Explore postings for jobs that interest you, note the educational and skills requirements, and check with your human resources department to see what is available.

If your company does not offer the training you need, you have other options.

- ☼ Can you learn a new skill simply by watching a coworker or mentor?
- ☼ Does a local community college or adult education center teach classes in what you need to learn?
- ☼ Consider online classes. With schools like NYU, Boston University, the University of Denver, and many others now offering online certification and graduate classes, online credits are becoming more and more acceptable to employers.
- ☼ Is there a book you can use to teach yourself at your own pace?

On the other hand, you may find that you need a graduate degree in business or education or another field. If this is the case, you'll have to consider local colleges or online programs, and talk with their staff to determine how you can make school a part of your schedule again. Today universities are working hard to accommodate the schedules of adult students by offering accelerated programs, weekend and evening classes, and online classrooms.

Paying Your Way

Unfortunately, to gain more education, you may have to pay for it. But you have options here as well:

☼ Remember that many companies offer at least partial tuition assistance for certain classes and degrees.

☼ While many grants and scholarships are offered primarily to undergraduates, adult students can still apply for financial aid through the state and federal governments, as well as third parties such as social clubs, religious groups, community groups, and so forth. (And you should apply for as many scholarships and grants as possible!)

☼ Those who have served or are serving in the military or military reserves can also tap into the GI bill for help.

☼ Many campuses allow students to pay out their tuition over the course of the semester for a small fee.

Nontraditional student scholarships are offered by many institutions of higher learning; qualifications may include age and circumstances such as career change, divorce, and single parenthood. There are many scholarship reference books and free Web sites, such as EducationPlanner.com, to help you find scholarships to apply for. (Avoid using services that charge you for searches and claim to "guarantee" or otherwise promise scholarship money in return.)

If you do not qualify for scholarships and grants, or your educational needs exceed them, you may need to apply for a loan.

Government loan programs, fortunately, are based on financial need (not just income), with *need* being defined as the difference between your educational costs and your ability to pay. So don't let your current income or potential tuition deter you from applying to schools that interest you.

If a federal program still isn't sufficient, or you do not qualify, you can arrange for a loan from a bank or credit union. Check with the student aid departments of schools you apply to first—some colleges may have an established lender arrangement or private loan program for their students.

Of course, we've left out one main reason to further your education—because you want to. If getting that master's degree in writing or even just learning how to play the guitar helps you better enjoy life, and you have the time and the means to pursue it, by all means do so. The best education, after all, is learning how to make yourself happy!

From the Desk of

Elizabeth Kanna
Dream Maker and Cofounder, Dream In You

My life changed in an instant eight years ago. While reading one night, I ran into a familiar quote, and its significance ignited a passion long forgotten in the hubbub of my daily life. Excited with my discovery, I grabbed a pen and paper and, until the sun declared the start of a new day for me, I captured the vision of what I wanted my life to be. This vision set in motion a personal and professional transformation that continues to empower and transform my life all these years later.

I'm often asked, *"How did you do it? How did you create your dream?"* That night I vowed to let passion guide, inspire, and shield that vision against the dream killers we all have: well-meaning friends, coworkers, life situations, lack of the "right" degree, and our own fear. No more would dream killers stop me from creating work that I was passionate about and that utilized my talents and gifts. Unless you are passionate about what you do, you'll never achieve true success in your career. Passion provides the power and conviction to break through any barriers that come your way. And if you're moving towards your dream, barriers will show up. Count on it.

And who doesn't take notice of an individual passionate about his or her work? If you decide to change employers or careers, your passion will set you apart from the pack. When you reach out to others for connections to that dream job, your passion will inspire them to help you as much as they can.

What is your next move? A great way to figure it out is to discover—or rediscover—your true passion. Try these exercises: Close your eyes, and in your mind and heart live your idea of a perfect day in which you're doing work you love. See every detail of that day. Think about inheriting $10 million. After several months (okay, maybe several years) of traveling, sitting on the beach, and playing, what would you do next? Hidden somewhere within these reflections is the key to your passion.

The quote that changed my life? "Go confidently in the direction of your dreams. Live the life you have imagined." —Henry David Thoreau

Dream in You is a pro-bono program that helps others create their dream jobs.

THINK Outside the Box

Odd Scholarships

Think you don't stand a chance at winning a scholarship? Take a look at some of these unusual undergrad grants:

- Ball State University (Muncie, IN) offers the $10,000 "David Letterman Scholarship" for outstanding creativity.

- Juniata College (Huntingdon, PA) makes available to left-handers two $1,000 scholarships every year.

- The Billy Barty Foundation, created by the diminutive, eponymous actor, offers scholarships to those under 4'10" and with a medical form of dwarfism.

- Meanwhile, Tall Clubs International has an annual scholarship award of $1,000 that goes to a graduating high school senior of tall stature (minimum height for females 5'10"; males 6'2") who meets, er, tall academic and character standards. Applicants must write an essay on "What Being Tall Means to Me." For more information, visit www.tall.org.

- The John Gatling Scholarship offers a full scholarship to North Carolina State University, and is named for the founder of the Gatling gun (but doesn't require any skill with a six-shooter).

- The Klingon (yes, as in *Star Trek*) Language Institute awards a $500 scholarship annually to a student seeking a degree in language study. (Fluency in Klingon not required.)

BENEFITS

You may have heard the phrase "golden handcuffs," referring to the perks that keep longtime workers stuck in jobs where they aren't happy—they can't leave without forfeiting valuable benefits, such as extended vacation time, bonuses, and pensions they've accumulated over the years.

You probably are not far enough along in your career to be so invested in any one company that you can't leave without regret. But you may have great benefits, even if you dislike your job, and are reluctant to give them up.

Good for you—benefits are a large and important part of your compensation package. (We'll discuss benefits in detail in chapter 9.) You don't want to make a move without first doing some research into the jobs and companies you are considering, and comparing what they offer to the benefits you currently have. Such benefits may include retirement plans, child care, tuition assistance, vacation time, and health care—a benefit whose costs have swelled in recent years both for employers and employees. Think about questions like these:

- ☼ Do the new companies you're considering offer you and your family comparable health insurance?
- ☼ Have you or a family member recently had a serious illness or injury requiring ongoing care? Although by law your new insurance company will have to cover you, certain treatments that your current plan offers may not be covered by your new plan. Your doctor might not be in the new company's network either.
- ☼ Are you prepared to go back to two weeks' vacation if you currently receive four?
- ☼ Are you enrolled in a training or degree program with your current company that you are better off finishing before making a move?

If certain benefits you now receive are important to you and your family, you may consider looking for a new position in your current company. At the very least, make sure to carefully investigate and understand the benefits offered by any company you interview with.

If you need help sorting through these issues, consider talking to a financial adviser, a spiritual leader, or a trusted friend. Also, your current company may have an Employee Assistance Program (EAP) through which you can get free advice as you sort out your next career steps.

LONG DAY'S JOURNEY INTO EMPLOYMENT

A final challenge you may face involves the duration of your job search. At this point in your career your search is most likely going to take longer than it used to—but for good reasons.

When you were looking for an entry-level job, you were willing to take whatever you could find to get your foot in the door. And while landing your first real job was nothing to sneeze at, you probably entered the workplace on the bottom rung with, let's face it, not a whole lot of responsibility. In other words, there wasn't a high level of risk for you or your company.

But now you are more selective in what you want in a job—and companies will be more selective in hiring employees at your level. According to various studies, it's not unusual for a job search to last four to six months. This holds true as you progress further down your career path: In 2004, outplacement firm Challenger, Gray & Christmas conducted a study of three thousand displaced managers and executives, and reported that most found new jobs within four months. (The good news: Almost 87 percent were given equivalent or better salaries at the new jobs.)

A company is looking for an employee it can keep around, who can take on more responsibility quickly, and potentially manage others right off the bat. For this reason, you may undergo several interviews for each job, meeting higher-level managers and executives (who, because *they* have more responsibility, may travel more and have fuller schedules with less time for interviews). There are more calls to references, more thorough background checks, even intelligence and personality testing before you get the nod.

Luckily, the time it takes for you to search also gives you time to think about what you really want. That way you're not making a knee-jerk decision—you're exploring different options and not just taking the first thing that comes along.

Finally, you want to begin looking beyond your current job search and think long term. This is your life—it's time to decide what you want to do with the rest of it, or at least the next year or two, and try to find a job that furthers your career path.

Remember when people used to ask you, "What do you want to be when you grow up?" Now that you are grown up, do those same things still interest you? What job can you get now to put you on the path to a wonderfully gratifying and fulfilling career?

It also may be time to revisit your dreams. Look down the road and reset goals. They may be entirely different from when you were just starting out.

In the end, keep in mind the blessings and unexpected dreams-come-true (spouse, good health, kids, and so on) you have in your life and let those ground you as you search.

Recommended Books

Personal Budgeting: An Easy, Smart Guide to Managing Your Money (Barnes & Noble Basics Series) by Barbara Wagner (Silver Lining Books, 2003, ISBN 0760737193, $9.95).

Saving Money (Barnes & Noble Basics Series) by Barbara Loos (Silver Lining Books, 2003, ISBN 0760740208, $9.95).

Cash for Grad School: The Ultimate Guide to Grad School Scholarships (Harperresource Book Series) by Cynthia Ruiz McKee & Phillip C. McKee (HarperCollins Publishers, 2004, ISBN 0688139566, $23.95).

Second Acts: Creating the Life You Really Want, Building the Career You Truly Desire by Stephen M. Pollan & Mark Levine (HarperCollins Publishers, 2003, ISBN 0060514884, $12.95).

The Complete Idiot's Guide to Managing Your Time by Jeff Davidson (Alpha, 2001, ISBN 0028642635, $16.95).

The 7 Habits of Highly Effective People by Steven R. Covey (The Free Press, 2004, ISBN 0743269519, $15.00).

Recommended Web Sites

Yahoo! Finance:
http://finance.yahoo.com

Yahoo! Finance Money Manager:
https://finance.secure.yahoo.com/box

Yahoo! Finance Planning Center:
http://planning.yahoo.com

Education Planner:
www.educationplanner.com

Sallie Mae:
www.salliemae.com

The Motley Fool—Financial news and tools:
www.fool.com

Find Your Spot—Quiz to help you find the best community for you:
www.findyourspot.com

CHAPTER 3

Opportunities Knocking: Open the Door to These Resources

"Opportunity knocking? Can you hold?"

We've all seen the clowns at the circus juggling first three, then four, five, or more balls at once. As if that's not stressful enough, then they add more dangerous objects to the group, like knives or chainsaws. They run back and forth, lunging, tossing and catching, sweating and straining, desperate to keep from dropping any objects.

Sound familiar?

You may feel a little overwhelmed trying to find a job while already *holding* a job, not to mention balancing family and other commitments. However, being currently employed can give you an edge over the competition; your work and life experience can provide many resources and opportunities to move forward.

Even if you're currently laid off and/or unemployed, you too have access to more help than you may realize.

In this chapter we'll take a look at these opportunities for people who have been in the workforce for a number of years, and how to capitalize on them to find your next job.

MENTORS

To paraphrase the Beatles, we get by with a little help from our friends.

Your network is always the best place to start when you're looking for a job—and why not aim high, at those with more experience than you? In and out of work you are surrounded by those people who can use their own mistakes and successes to guide you.

Whether your company has a formal mentoring program or you have a higher-up you can trust, there may be people right in your own company who can give you advice on making your next career move. (If not, consider talking to a colleague in your industry but outside your company.)

If you want to stay with your company but move to a different job, finding a mentor will help you better position yourself to do that. (And taking the initiative to step up and ask for help in making your next move might give you an edge in getting one of those jobs.)

If you want to leave the company altogether, your mentor can use his or her experience to advise you about what path might best suit you, what your strengths and weaknesses are, and what he thinks you can do to improve.

For example, Adam couldn't decide between two potential job offers. Both were similar in pay and responsibility, but on opposite sides of the country. Having lived in his current city for five years, he was excited about the prospect of relocating, yet reluctant to make the move.

He asked his mentor, John, a more senior colleague in a different department, for help. John explained that Adam's worries were perfectly natural, but he had no reason to fear relocating at this point in his life, stating, "You can't seriously mess up your career before you're thirty." While his words were said somewhat in jest, they clarified Adam's thinking. He accepted the job that appealed to him most, relocated, and never looked back.

But won't asking about my career path be a red flag that I am looking to leave? you may ask.

Not necessarily. Ask for advice in a broad sense. Present your case this way: "I'm thinking ahead about where I can go next careerwise, and would love your feedback on some options I've been considering." Offer to take your mentor to lunch or even just coffee. Keep it informal and let her know how much you respect her opinion. After all, that's why you are seeking her help.

Throughout this book we discuss ways to keep your job search private—however, there are times you'll need to discuss your thoughts with someone else. While we don't recommend broadcasting your decision around the company, hopefully your mentor is trustworthy enough that you can be completely honest with him. Even if that mentor is your current manager, a good manager will want you to feel fulfilled in your current position, and not be offended that you are thinking long term. If you have a strong relationship with your manager, don't be afraid to approach her with questions about your career path—you may already have discussed these issues in performance reviews. Without stating that you want to leave, ask about ways you can grow in your department and take on more responsibility. Communicate the skills you'd like to develop further. You may find that you have more opportunities at your current company than you think. And if not, at least you asked—now you can begin looking elsewhere without worrying that you might be overlooking a new position at your current company.

Remember, *everyone* changes jobs and for a variety of reasons. You may be happy but have outgrown your position. Or maybe your spouse has found a great opportunity in California and you need to go with her. Whatever your reason, share as much or as little information as you are comfortable with—just find someone you admire, who can give you solid advice in your best interest, not the company's.

Meanwhile, even if you are unemployed, you still have mentors you can work with. Consider calling one of your references for lunch and some brainstorming. Talk to family members, former employers, or professors—anyone who knows you and your talents and can assess you more objectively than you can assess yourself. While these contacts may not have jobs to give you, they can at least encourage you and maybe point out some options you hadn't considered before.

From the Desk of

Keith Ferrazzi
CEO, Ferrazzi Greenlight

From a career standpoint, it's everyone's worst nightmare. You wake up one day after years of loyal service. You go to work and all you see is a bunch of freshly minted MBAs flying past you on the career track. Someone at the water cooler comments, "They're just getting the promotions because they know the boss."

Well, of course they do! And you have to, also! It's not illegal, nor is it impossible, for you to get access to the people who make decisions in your organization—to get them to care enough about you to invest time into making you a success, and to get the opportunities to demonstrate your competence on work that really matters. No, it's mandatory. And the secret password to getting such access, care, and opportunity is mentorship.

The best thing you can do for your career right now is to find mentors. Seek mentors inside your company, inside and outside of your division. Seek mentors outside your company, too. And remember, a successful mentoring relationship needs equal parts utility and emotion. You can't simply ask somebody to be personally invested in you. There has to be some reciprocity involved—whether it's hard work or loyalty that you give in return—that gets someone to invest in you in the first place. Then, when the process kicks in, you have to mold your mentor into a coach; someone for whom your success is in some small or big way his success.

No matter when you plan to make your next career move, start finding mentors now. The point is to build the relationships before you need them, so whenever that next big opportunity comes along, the people who make decisions are the same people who care most about your success.

Keith Ferrazzi is the author of Never Eat Alone: And Other Secrets to Success, One Relationship at a Time *(www.NeverEatAlone.com).*

HUMAN RESOURCES

Like mentors, some of the best resources for a new job can be right there in your own company, where all jobs start—in the human resources department.

If anyone knows about available jobs in your company, it's the human resources department. They also know about helping employees find fulfilling work (with confidentiality). If you're struggling with your current job, want some advice about your next step, or want to know what other opportunities are available at your company, speak with your human resources representative. He or she can give you advice and insight on whether your current company is the place for you long term.

For example, the rep could help you set up formal or informal interviews with other managers at your workplace to learn more about opportunities in other departments. (Depending on your company's policy, you may need to divulge this information to your current manager.) The rep also knows about training programs where you can improve your skills.

Approaching HR worked for Sherry. She liked her company but had outgrown her executive assistant position. After finishing computer training courses, she hoped to transition to IT services—but she didn't know how to go about finding a job in that department. She went to her HR rep for help, and although it was another six months before a job opened up, Sherry was the first to know—and she got the job.

PROFESSIONAL ASSOCIATIONS

Professional associations (such as the American Association for the Advancement of Science, the Society of Professional Journalists, or the Travel Industry Association of America) are wonderful outlets for learning more about your field and jobs within it. Meetings and social events make you more visible in your industry, and give you a chance to meet other people in your field and learn what their jobs are like at other companies. You might even hear about job openings before they are posted. In addition, educational opportunities offered through these associations and insights gained through their publications provide you with knowledge that can make you more valuable in the marketplace.

Professional associations tend to require dues and certain career prerequisites (for example, you may need to be a full-time journalist or a veterinarian). But your current company may pay for your membership, and it's a great idea to take advantage of this perk.

If you are unemployed, you can still join professional associations—the dues will just have to come out of your pocket. But the opportunities are almost always worth the expense! Also, there are other business and community groups you can join for little or no money that can help you in your job search—the Chamber of Commerce, the Kiwanis Club, the Jaycees, and so on. We'll discuss these groups in more detail in chapter 4.

BUSINESS PUBLICATIONS

Many industries and professions have their own magazines and journals. They can be wide-ranging *(Money, Fast Company, Journal of the American Medical Association)* or more specific *(CIO Magazine, Writer's Digest, Male Nurse Magazine)*. Here you can find the latest news and trends in your field, including which companies are growing and launching new products and services. In addition, these journals offer tips to better your skills and lists of classes, seminars, and networking events—not to mention those little snippets of information you can use in a cover letter or interview to show that you really know your stuff.

Chances are your company already subscribes to the publications in your field. Check the company library or research center, and if they don't have what you need, consider asking your company to pay for a subscription for you. If you are unemployed, you can find most major industry publications at your public library or adult education/career center. Oftentimes, much of their content can be found free of charge on the Internet.

TRAINING/EDUCATION

We discussed in chapter 2 the value of furthering your training or education—especially if your company offers on-site training or tuition assistance. A degree, particularly an advanced one, can be a great boost. According to the *Occupational Outlook Handbook*, a bachelor's degree or higher is a foundation for all but one of the fifty highest-paying occupations. Karen Holbrook, now president of Ohio State University, pointed out in a 2001 speech: "The average national age for a master's degree student is thirty-three. Many of them come out of the workforce to enter a graduate program either full-time or part-time, usually to obtain a new credential that will help them in their careers, either by gaining additional training or upgrading their degrees."

But you don't necessarily need an advanced degree to get a better job. In the OOH's predictions for the twenty fastest growing occupations, a bachelor's or associate's degree is the most significant source of education or training for half of them. Also according to the OOH, marketing managers, financial managers, and even *aerospace engineers* make what are considered "very high" earnings but only *require* a bachelor's degree and perhaps some work experience.

Betsy had been a teacher for five years, but wanted to move into an administrative position. She went back to school for her MBA and used her degree to become an assistant principal at the same school where she had worked. It took Betsy two years, and it may take longer than that for you, but if you find that additional training or another degree would be beneficial in landing a better job, and you have the time and financial resources, definitely try to gain that expertise or credential.

hot facts

Education Pays...

Consider the following unemployment rates and earnings for full-time wage and salary workers, age twenty-five and over, by educational attainment (according to the Bureau of Labor Statistics):

Unemployment rate in 2003 (%)	Education attained	Median weekly earnings in 2003 ($)
2.1	Doctoral degree	1,349
1.7	Professional degree	1,307
2.9	Master's degree	1,064
3.3	Bachelor's degree	900
4.0	Associate's degree	672
5.2	Some college, no degree	622
5.5	High school graduate	554
8.8	Some high school, no diploma	396

BUSINESS TRAVEL

While the term *business travel* may make you groan, business trips offer you a number of advantages if you are searching for a new job.

First, the trips give you a chance to see new cities—at no cost to you. You can even tack on a weekend to sightsee and get a feel for whether a city is right for you.

Next, you get to visit other companies and check out their corporate cultures, what people at your level in similar jobs are doing and if they are happy, and what their workload is like. The same job can vary greatly from one company to another, so while you may be unhappy in sales for your pharmaceutical company, you might find that selling outdoor equipment is much more exciting. Or you might learn about jobs in your industry that you didn't know existed.

Business trips are also great networking opportunities. You never know who you will meet. So instead of doing the crossword puzzle, consider introducing yourself to the executive sitting next to you in the terminal—and get a business card! (However, use discretion—it's a small world, and there's a chance the guy next to you might know your boss.)

For example, Ryan worked for a printing company and attended an industry conference out of town. As part of the conference, there was a table where hopefuls could leave their resumes in folders designated for open jobs. Not only did Ryan score an interview right there at the conference, he got the job soon after.

Perhaps best of all, business travel can give you something you can't get at home—quiet time alone. You can work on your resume in the privacy of your hotel room, make calls to potential employers, even go on interviews if there is time, and all without a boss looking over your shoulder, a dog barking, or a kid waiting to be picked up from soccer practice. Obviously, your priority is to do your company's work first, but once that's done, it's your time to use as you please.

JOB FAIRS

Job fairs are large gatherings of companies' human resources representatives for the purpose of getting to know you and explaining their current or pending job openings.

While many of the jobs available at fairs tend to be junior or entry-level positions, it never hurts to go. They are usually free and put you face to face with recruiters from multiple companies who also might be hiring at your level. (Don't be intimidated if you're surrounded by college students and recent grads at a job fair. Your age and life experience may set you apart in recruiters' minds.) You can find out about job fairs through your local employment agency, news-papers, television, radio, job Web sites—and, of course, a Yahoo! search.

Job fairs are also a fantastic way to practice your interviewing skills if it's been some time since you've had a job interview. Because you only get a couple of minutes with each company's recruiter, you are forced to hone your personal **"elevator speech,"** a business term for concisely describing your high points and skills in less than a minute—as if you were fortunate enough to share an elevator ride with the hiring manager.

Some career fairs are general and feature all types of jobs. Others are for a specific field, such as teaching. We recommend that you go to as many as you can, even if you're not certain about which field to pursue, because there will still be a variety of jobs available.

Also, be open to exploring different companies and different industries. You never know—a local accounting firm might have a great marketing position available. A nursing home chain might need a Web site developer. Talk to any and every recruiter you can.

take a memo

All's "Fair"

Here are some practical tips for preparing for a job fair:

- ☼ Job fairs usually list the companies that will be attending. Research these companies ahead of time.

- ☼ For job fairs that occur on weekdays, avoid the lunch hour, when many other employed job seekers will stop by. Go earlier in the morning or later in the afternoon.

- ☼ Practice your greeting and your elevator speech in the mirror beforehand.

- ☼ Dress professionally; however, keep in mind that if you're going into the office earlier or later that day, and you work in a more casual environment, you should be careful not to draw attention to your attire (see page 143).

- ☼ Bring more copies of your resume than you think you will need.

Finally, when you're at the fair, try this handy tip: To "warm up," first go to a couple of booths you are fairly certain you are uninterested in. Practice with those recruiters before you move on to your preferred job opportunities. This will help you calm your nerves and polish your presentation.

THIRD-PARTY RECRUITERS

Another great option for the midcareer job seeker is to turn to a third-party recruiter. This group includes staffing firm recruiters and those recruiters typically referred to as *headhunters*.

Staffing Agencies: More Than Minimum Wage

Staffing agencies allow you to try on a job before you buy. These firms have graduated from the term "temp agencies" because many of them help employers find entry-level workers or trained professionals in fields like creative services, law, marketing, health care, and many more—and for permanent, not just short-term, jobs.

Signing on with a staffing agency lets you explore different facets of jobs you like in different company settings—frequently large, well-known companies. Often you can schedule fewer hours than the standard forty-hour workweek. If you aren't happy, you can leave after your term (usually two to three months) is up; if you love it, you could be hired by the company full time, or apply for other jobs you see posted in that company's roster of openings.

Staffing agencies make their money by charging employers a fee that is a percentage of your hourly pay. The agency will negotiate your rate for you—and a growing number provide benefits as well.

The downsides? Because staffing agencies take a big slice of the pie, companies *really* want quality when they employ someone placed by the agency. Only the most qualified job seekers will survive—people who can easily enter a new environment and hit the ground running. If you're at that level, there's a chance you'll make more money (the percentage that would have gone to the staffing agency) finding a job on your own.

For some people, the instability of temporary jobs can be frustrating and isolating. Yet others enjoy the change of scenery and the flexibility that staffing agencies offer. Take the case of Krista, a graphic designer and artist in Frederick, Maryland, who says: "I'll never work full time for one company again. Through a creative services staffing firm, I got assignments to work three days a week for a nonprofit and one day for a trade association, so I have an extra day to take art classes or just paint at home. I could make a little more money if I worked more hours, but this way I have more time to pursue the personal side of my work so I don't get burned out drawing medical diagrams. I've been doing this for two years and I love it."

From the Desk of

Roy Krause
President and CEO, Spherion Corporation

The concept of providing value is a key factor in business and in your career. Whether you are currently out of work, thinking about changing jobs, or vying for that next promotion, it's crucial that you assess the value you provide to your current and prospective employers and find ways to increase and promote your net value.

The key to increasing your professional value is to know what employers need and ensure the skills you have can grow as the industry, technology, and marketplace evolve. Adopting a grow-or-go mentality will help you stay on top of the learning curve, developing and fine-tuning the skills employers demand.

To keep pace with the skills evolution, consider joining and taking leadership roles in professional organizations which are focused on monitoring the trends and events affecting your profession. Look for opportunities to diversify your own skills by taking on tasks that are outside your job description. Join special project teams and ask to be a part of strategic initiatives in order to increase your experience. Consider taking evening or weekend classes to gain additional degrees or certifications, or simply to augment your existing skills.

Lastly, put a plan together to get on or move up the management track. Managers take on greater responsibility in the workplace and, as a result, can build their net value as employees. Find a mentor, either within your organization or through professional affiliations. It is also worth-while to look into management training programs and talk to employers about the traits, skills, and prerequisites for management consideration.

Most importantly, you must sell your value. The key to increasing your net worth is to understand the value you can offer and then to promote it in the right way. Try to quantify that value, preferably in ways that are measurable and that impact the bottom line of the organization.

Ultimately, your goal is to convince the employer that your perceived or potential value is greater than your perceived or potential costs. When you invest the time and energy into building your net worth, you will be in control of your next career move.

Spherion Corporation is a staffing and recruiting company based in Florida.

Finally, if a company wants to hire you after your temp job, you must really have impressed the decision makers—they have to pay an additional "finder's fee" to hire you away from the temp agency.

Headhunters

"Inside recruiters" work on salary within one company to find new talent. There are also "outside recruiters," or *headhunters*—those who work individually or, more often, for recruiting firms that are contracted by a company specifically to fill one or more positions. Some firms recruit for general jobs; others are more specific, focusing on a particular occupational field or fields (such as accounting or IT) or a specific industry (such as health care or financial services).

Despite the scary-sounding nickname, these headhunters can help you. While executive recruiters place only those who earn well over $200,000, any experienced worker can use an outside recruiter. (You may even have gotten a call from one already.) Contacting an outside recruiter is similar to contacting an inside recruiter at a company; however, there are some small differences to keep in mind.

Outside recruiters make their money by placing people. Although they do make an effort to learn about a company's culture and what personalities would best fit there, they are most interested in the list of skills they have been given to find—and whether or not you have them. So be upfront and very clear about your skills and the type of job you seek in your cover letter and resume.

As Darrell W. Gurney states in his book, *Headhunters Revealed: Career Secrets for Choosing and Using Professional Recruiters*: "Recruiters are already fixated on certain clients and positions they are trying to fill—their eyes almost filter everything else out . . . so don't break your neck over a cover letter to a headhunter. . . . Save yourself a lot of time by providing the minimal information a headhunter usually wants to know up front." Therefore, unlike with standard cover letters, you will want to state your salary history and preferences. This will help you and the recruiter find each other. (For more on cover letters and resumes, see chapters 6 and 7.)

As with certain job postings, not every recruiter is legitimate. Don't give any money to recruiters—they are paid by a *company*, not by you. Finally, even if a recruiter doesn't have any positions for you at this time, he might down the road. So once you establish a relationship with a recruiter, you should maintain it through occasional e-mails and by passing on names of others who might be looking for jobs the recruiter is trying to fill.

take a **memo**

Ask the Expert: Job Searching

Here are some of the steps job seekers can take to increase their chances of identifying and landing a good position—courtesy of David L. Dunkel, Chairman and CEO of Kforce Professional Staffing:

- **Define what's most important to you.** The right company will be one whose values mesh with yours.

- **Move beyond a narrow industry focus.** Specific industry needs can change rapidly, and the most successful individuals can transfer their skills readily to other industries.

- **Understand the impact the economy has on the job search.** Identify the current hiring climate in the industries being targeted, as well as indicators for future career growth.

- **Consider a contract or temporary assignment.** Such assignments can provide advantages over permanent employment such as flexible hours and broader experience in a shorter period of time. Some staffing firms pay a premium for skilled consultants and provide excellent benefits. Temporary assignments can also be a great way to get your foot in the door with a premier employer.

- **Upgrade your skills...constantly.** This applies to both hard and soft skills. Individuals who pay attention to ongoing professional and personal development demonstrate initiative as well as higher skill levels.

- **Consider a mix of job search channels.** The best strategy is to take advantage of many job search methods including networking, job boards, job fairs, company Web postings, and a staffing firm that specializes in your area of expertise.

Some final thoughts: Midcareer job seekers should consider the long-term picture. The goal should be to position oneself for long-term economic security, rather than looking for positions that will simply pay the most in the short term. They should seek roles that fit their values and career goals. Individuals who become "job mercenaries" often destroy their careers in the long run.

Employment and Outplacement Agencies

While employment agencies are available to any job seeker, they can be particularly helpful if you are unemployed. These centers offer many services—career counseling, classes, testing, and information on job opportunities. And they are free—so use them!

If you have been laid off, you may already be familiar with your local and state employment agencies, which help you obtain unemployment benefits. You should also know that places like community centers and adult education centers offer training and career counseling.

Outplacement agencies are private companies that give unemployed professionals advice on how to land another job. Sometimes companies will retain outplacement agencies to help newly laid-off employees get back on their feet. The services are part of the severance package and include everything from counseling to resume writing to office and Internet access. If these services are available to you, be sure to take advantage of them.

Career Counselors

Private career counselors offer career training, resume-writing services, job counseling, and vocational testing—not to mention personal support. Many have formal training in psychology as well. They can be pricey, but if you have the means, a career counselor can help you focus and set goals—just be sure to find one who is licensed, does not guarantee to find you a job, and does not charge you upfront.

Visit the National Board of Certified Counselors' "CounselorFind" tool to find reputable counselors.

Internships

Sometimes you just want to try on a job for size. Internships—short-term, usually unpaid positions—let you do just that. For example, perhaps you are a photographer who would like to work as a network news cameraman. An unpaid internship at a local news station might help you get the skills you need and give you a chance to figure out if the job is right for you.

Worried that you're too busy with the kids or other obligations to take on unpaid work? Because internships pay little or no salary, you may have some flexibility in working as an intern—say, three hours a week or one night a week.

And internships give you a great shot at a job offer. A 2004 survey of companies who used interns, conducted by the National Association of Colleges and Employers, found that about 45 percent of them filled full-time staff positions from their intern pools.

While this survey was conducted with recent college grads in mind, it still shows the value of internship experience.

THINK Outside the Box

Internships: Not Just for College Kids Anymore

You may think internships are only open to college students, but anyone can apply for an internship—you just need the right attitude.

The most desirable candidates are eager to learn and do not mind taking direction from others—regardless of age. Internships, after all, are designed for people with little or no experience. But those who do take the chance to get a foot in the door of their dream career usually find that it's worth it.

Better yet, because of your experience and confidence level, you already know how to interact in a workplace setting. This gives you a leg up in learning the skills you need.

INFORMATIONAL INTERVIEWS

Informational interviews—informal conversations with those experienced in particular fields—are one of the most productive yet least-utilized tools for job seekers. To find out exactly what is involved in a job, you should go straight to the source. And for once, *you* get to do the interviewing!

You may feel awkward approaching another working adult and asking for help, but you don't have to meet with a company president. Someone in a position similar to one you would like to hold might be easier for you to approach and better able to give you information about the job you're seeking and the field itself.

Informational interviews also give you a chance to practice your interviewing skills in a more relaxed environment. Yes, you should still dress professionally, and yes, you should still research the company where your interviewee works and come prepared with appropriate questions. You should also be ready to give a quick synopsis of your relevant skills and experience. You should even bring a resume or two (but offer it only with the polite request of "placing it on file for future consideration"). Because there is no job on the line, this is your chance to ask the big questions about the position and about how your skills might or might not fit into it, and get real answers from someone who knows.

(While we can't promise anything, remember that job and internship offers do sometimes come from informational interviews.)

▶ **Action Items:** Information, Please?

Make a list of three people/companies you would like to interview, and contact them about informational interviews.

1._____

    Phone number (   )_____ - _____
    E-mail _____

2._____

    Phone number (   )_____ - _____
    E-mail _____

3._____

    Phone number (   )_____ - _____
    E-mail _____

Prepare for the informational interviews by:

- ☼ Reading about the field and the company
- ☼ Noting why your interests and skills have drawn you toward this field
- ☼ Making a list of questions, such as:
  - What is a typical day like?
  - What degrees do you hold, and have they helped you in this field?
  - What is the most important skill I need for a job in this field?
  - How else would you recommend I bolster my skills for a job in this field?
  - How did this job differ from your expectations?

Employee Assistance Programs (EAPs)

Your current company may have what is known as an Employee Assistance Program, or EAP. These wonderful services are networks of health care and counseling professionals who can assist employees with everything from the death of a loved one to adopting a child to—of course—changing jobs. They are confidential, free, and often on-site.

Passive Job Seekers

Finally, even being currently employed is something of an opportunity. You have the luxury of being what is called a passive job seeker. In other words, you can post your resume online, set up your e-mail agents, and then wait for employers to come to you! You also have more time to evaluate jobs as they come in for salary, working conditions, ease of commute, and so forth.

However, you can improve your chances considerably if you become more visible in your industry. Even if you're unemployed, you can still speed up the job search process by raising your profile among your peers. For example, you can contribute articles to a magazine or newsletter in your industry. You can speak at events, or start your own networking groups. You can even teach classes at your local community center or house of worship. You'll probably have to do it for free, but it's a chance to get yourself on people's radar screens—particularly those of recruiters—and it gives you more fodder for your resume.

Whether you choose to try everything on this list or you simply sit down with one mentor for feedback, using the opportunities we have described in this chapter will help you take charge of your own job search and take the next steps on your career path.

Recommended Books

Making the Most of Being Mentored by Gordon F. Shea (Course Technology, Inc., 1999, ISBN 1560525460, $13.95).

The Princeton Review Best 109 Internships, Mark Oldman & Samer Hamadeh (Random House Information Group, 2003, ISBN 0375763198, $21.00).

The Internship Bible, 2005 Edition, Mark Oldman & Samer Hamadeh (Random House Information Group, 2005, ISBN 0375764682, $25.00).

Vault Guide to Top Internships (Vault Career Library Series), Samer Hamadeh, Mark Oldman, & Marcy Lerner (Vault, Inc., 2004, ISBN 1581312911, $14.95).

Recommended Web Sites

The Internet Public Library—Associations on the Net:
www.ipl.org/div/aon

National Board of Certified Counselors:
www.nbcc.org

International Volunteer Programs Association:
www.volunteerinternational.org

Ask the Headhunter:
www.asktheheadhunter.com

CHAPTER 4

People Who Need People: Care and Feeding of Your Network

"IT ISN'T WHAT YOU KNOW. IT'S WHO YOU KNOW"

Networking—kind of a fancy word for making friends and contacts, isn't it?

But networking is a critical process—maybe the most important element of your job search: The Society of Human Resources Management (and almost every career expert you talk to) estimates that **60–80 percent of jobs are filled through word-of-mouth**.

So the more *mouths* you have around to give you the *word* about jobs, the better. Like the old party game "Six Degrees of Kevin Bacon," you might be surprised at the odd connection that leads you to your goal. The woman next to you in line at the bank could be a tech guru, an executive, or the human resources director for your favorite sports team.

But you already have a huge network, even if you haven't put it to good use yet. In addition to the family and friends who helped you when you were first starting your job search, now you have many more business contacts—vendors, clients, customers, and colleagues. You also have more opportunities to expand your network further.

In this chapter, we'll look at how to make the most of the contacts you already have, as well as ways to connect with new people who can give you good leads on jobs.

take a **memo**

What Is SHRM?

The Society for Human Resource Management (SHRM) is the world's largest association devoted to the field. With nearly 200,000 members, SHRM is dedicated to providing comprehensive resources to the human resources community and to ensure that HR personnel are informed and effective in developing and educating companies' staffs.

SHRM (www.shrm.org) follows trends in hiring and management of staff as well as recognizing companies with diverse and innovative approaches to hiring. It's a wonderful resource if you want to know, for example, the latest news on corporate health care coverage, or the best small-to-medium-size companies to work for, or you'd simply like some valuable insight from recruiters on how you can become better at interviewing and writing resumes. Much of the site's content is available for free online.

WHY YOU SHOULD NET A NETWORK

If you've ever left a cupcake on the ground after a picnic, you've seen one of nature's greatest examples of networking—ants. They live in colonies, march in groups, and work together to transport food, construct their homes, and protect each other.

In other words, even nature's tiniest critters understand that there is safety in numbers. So before we go on, let's review some crucial ways that growing your network can help you.

Time and Again

Worried about job hunting while working and managing a family? Tap into your network to save yourself time! Sometimes a fellow alumnus, a neighbor, or a business colleague can "get you in" so you can circumvent much of the red tape other applicants have to go through—like submitting their resumes to databases and trying to impress recruiters (who are sizing up other candidates in the meantime)—before they reach the hiring manager. By putting you directly in touch with people making the hiring decisions, your network saves you *time*—time you can use to seek other jobs or spend with loved ones.

Employers Trust Them

Imagine that you have to select a pediatrician. Who would you rather choose—a stranger or someone referred to you by one of your closest friends?

Employers trust networks because they take some of the unknown out of the hiring equation. The hiring manager has a lot of pressure to find the right workers—bad hires can be extremely costly. Anything (or, rather, *anyone*) that proves your worth helps the hiring manager feel more confident about you as a potential hire.

This is especially true when your advocate is already employed at a company where you'd like to work. A current employee knows you as well as the company culture and whether or not you'd make a good fit. Having this person endorse you can move your resume to the top of the hiring manager's pile.

The Inside Scoop

Let's say your mother-in-law gives you a heads-up about a job at her company. (So maybe you don't want to work with your mother-in-law, but at least now you have a lead on a job.) If you hear about a job from someone you know, you have a chance to apply for it before the job is even posted. Better yet, your contact can personally hand your resume to the recruiter or hiring manager. This gives you an edge over other applicants—as we mentioned, someone who knows you is vouching for you. You can also find out more details about the position that you can use to tailor your resume and cover letter.

take a memo

No Network? No Excuses!

Let's look at some reasons why people don't keep up their networks, and why their reasoning is flawed:

I hate talking to people; I'm too shy. Yes, networking forces you to meet and talk to people—but that's never a bad skill to cultivate. You can always use it on the job, say, for pitching a big idea to an executive. Start with people who may be outside your chosen industry—talk to waiters, the mailman, bank tellers—and then graduate to people who can help your career.

Isn't networking really just "schmoozing"? It can be, if it's done insincerely. Think of the *person* first, not what she can do for you. Listen to her, learn about her, and view networking as a mutual relationship where you help each other.

Networking takes too much time—I need to find a job now! Sure, anything worth doing well takes time. But networking also *saves* you time—time spent customizing cover letters for jobs for which you're not a good fit. Time spent searching your favorite companies' Web sites for jobs that exist but are only posted internally. Time spent interviewing at companies whose cultures are too restrictive for you. A network can circumvent all these missteps and more.

Lean on Me

Networks not only provide you with support and encouragement, but they give you a sounding board for ideas and suggestions. You can learn from your contacts' experiences. You can use them to help you practice making your personal pitch and answering interview questions—or just help you decide which shoes go with which skirt. Most important, they will give you a lift when you're feeling discouraged.

Networks can also help life in general go a little more smoothly—never a bad thing when you're conducting a job search. Trust your network to recommend doctors, lawyers, child care professionals, or even a good sushi restaurant. For the same reason, products have celebrity endorsements: You are more willing to trust something referred to you by someone you know.

EXPANDING YOUR NETWORK

You may think that you already have enough friends and contacts, and there's no need to worry about widening your network.

But to network effectively as an experienced worker, you need to begin reaching beyond your usual circle of friends and colleagues. Let's consider an example of networking with people you don't consider business "contacts." Say you are currently a junior corporate marketing executive hoping to find a job doing marketing for a nonprofit organization. You let three people know about your aspirations:

1) Ron, an accountant at your former company who always shared your interest in skydiving

2) Sean, your next-door neighbor

3) Leigh, an acquaintance from your daily bus ride

Ron calls his cousin, Sarah, the vice president of a nonprofit in Seattle. There are no job openings at her agency right now, but Sarah just met another nonprofit executive at a community event and remembers that he was looking to hire a marketing person.

Meanwhile, Sean gives your resume to the head of a nonprofit for which he volunteers. There is a job available in communications—not your specialty, but it still involves getting the agency's message across to the public.

Finally, Leigh's brother-in-law used to work for a nonprofit and still stays in touch with his former coworkers. She takes a copy of your resume to give to him.

So there—just by talking to three people outside your usual network, you already have leads on three potential jobs. Finding leads won't always go this smoothly, but once you start spreading the word, you never know what you'll hear back in two weeks, two months, or even two years. So let people know about your interests, stay in touch with them, and keep them posted on your progress.

From the Desk of

John Kaestle
President and CEO, Vanson HaloSource, Inc.

Several years ago, I had the opportunity to make a journey. Not a trip, but an adventure—a journey into learning about a business community, meeting key leaders, understanding their businesses, and making friends and developing a network that ultimately resulted in full-time employment. It was real work, occupying every day—as well as evenings and weekends—with reading and studying, just like a job. So what did I learn along the way? Three things:

You need a plan and a strategy. You have no chance without some careful thought about your goals and aspirations, your "value proposition" or "what makes you unique," your values and personal needs, and your family. How else do you respond to basic questions like, "So tell me about yourself," "What are you looking for?" or "What makes you special or different?" With that said, remember to be flexible and avoid unnecessary constraints. You never know what the next opportunity will look like.

Most jobs are not advertised; they're not even "open." You want to meet, network, and sell yourself to as many key decision makers as possible. Make the right connection and they will figure it out. The opportunity will find you.

And yes, it is best thought of as real work, because it is. The skills are the same skills you would employ to be effective in business: organization, preparation, communications, creativity, perseverance, and a sense of humor. Expect to get up early, stay late, wait patiently in reception areas, and always be courteous and respectful. Remember, it's real work to find work.

Vanson HaloSource is a bioscience company that creates innovative solutions for a wide range of customer applications.

▶**Action Items:** Casting a Wide Net

List at least one person in each of the following categories who could serve as a member of your personal network:

- Family _____

- Friends _____

- Alumni _____

- Former Professors _____

- Neighbors _____

- Former Employers _____

- Volunteer Organizations _____

- House of Worship _____

- Former Colleagues _____

- Occasional/Incidental Contacts (your financial adviser, manicurist, yoga instructor, etc.) _____

MAKING NEW CONTACTS

We've discussed how to build on contacts you already have in order to find jobs; now let's look at some ways to make new contacts.

Business Associations and Events

As we discussed in chapter 3, there are business associations for just about every field you could imagine. If you are not a member already, you should be. Look for associations in your industry (for example, the Society of Professional Journalists or the American Bar Association) as well as community groups like the Chamber of Commerce or Kiwanis. One popular group is Toastmasters, a business club that focuses on teaching its members good public speaking skills.

Business associations offer endless networking possibilities. Social events, trade shows, and conferences let you meet other people in your field and learn about the corporate culture at other companies, not to mention give you a chance to find out about job openings in the field.

So, whether it's a happy hour in your own company or a convention across the country, take advantage of every business event you can. Why? Because they:

- ☼ Introduce you to other people in your field.
- ☼ Put you in direct contact with speakers and other executives without having to go through e-mail or assistants to reach them.
- ☼ Offer settings in which it is perfectly natural to ask about someone's company and job description, as well as trade business cards.

Be sure to make the most of these events. Go to the workshops, and if there is a dinner afterwards, don't miss it—attend and get to know your tablemates. An hour at a meal can immediately score you five or six new contacts in your industry. When you engage in conversation with fellow event-goers, remember to ask questions and demonstrate your knowledge of your field. And don't forget to *follow up*, within three to five days if possible, with an e-mail or a phone call. Keep the business cards you collect, making notes about each person on the back. Stay in contact with those who can help you get a leg up—and be sure to reciprocate!

Networking Groups and Job Clubs

These groups, like Boston's Monday Network or Businesspersons Between Jobs in St. Louis, exist for the express purpose of helping their members find jobs. Some are general job-seeking groups, while others are geared toward a specific occupation, industry, or career stage.

If you're shy or unsure about how to get started, structured networking groups may be the answer for you. With the help of facilitators, employed peers, and career coaches, these groups offer opportunities for members to connect and share job leads. Structured networking groups teach networking techniques in a safe, nonthreatening forum. They are usually organized by profession, income, or geography.

You'll have to do some research to find the group that's right for you. Perform a search using Yahoo! to find groups close by. Another great resource is the Riley Guide's networking resource Web site. Or you can start a group of your own!

Web Communities

Like the in-person groups we've been discussing, virtual online communities offer valuable job information and advice. Use Web chat rooms and job boards like Yahoo! Groups and Yahoo! HotJobs Communities to "talk" with other job seekers. Also consider online networking groups such as LinkedIn, for example, an online network of more than three million professionals across the world. Jobster, an invitation-only networking site, connects professionals and employers through referrals. And even more social sites like Friendster can offer valuable networking opportunities.

Not only do online communities help you build your network, but oftentimes recruiters scour these professional communities searching for qualified candidates.

Alumni Groups and Events

Alumni groups are wonderful networking tools because their members forge an instant bond based on shared history, good times, bad times, or just bad professors. You can find common ground with a fellow alumnus simply because you lived in the same dormitory, even if he listened to Hip-Hop and you listened to Sheryl Crow. Reach out to those on the alumni list, and keep your contact information updated.

It's easy to find alumni in your area—just check your school/organization Web site or call the alumni office. You can get together with alumni for purely social purposes or for informational interviews.

Organized alumni social gatherings, such as monthly dinners, seminars, or volunteer events, make for fun networking opportunities. These help you meet people in a more informal setting and can be preferable for introverts who feel uncomfortable approaching people directly about jobs.

Even if your college doesn't have a local alumni chapter, consider attending the next big event in a nearby city, if applicable.

Volunteer Groups

Volunteering is a wonderful way to network. Not only are you meeting like-minded people, but you're also learning new skills that you can apply to the real world.

Midcareer professionals, in particular, can tap their skills in ways that give them opportunities to interact with other professionals. For example, a lawyer can offer to do pro bono work for a nonprofit. An office manager can assist in organizing a charity gala. A consultant and triathlete can coach for a charitable endeavor like the Leukemia and Lymphoma Society's "Team-in-Training" marathon/triathlon programs.

Shorter-term commitments, like New York Cares Day, in which participants help out for one day building playgrounds or painting schools, can also yield job leads. You never know who'll be planting roses next to you—it could be the CEO of a telecom company or the recruiter for your favorite snack food manufacturer.

And volunteering can lead directly to jobs. For example, Linda had been working as a volunteer for a local dog rescue group. A woman who adopted a dog from the group also happened to run her own interior design business. When the new dog owner got to know Linda and found out about her training in interior design, she interviewed her—and hired her!

 **THINK Outside the Box**

Alternative Ways to Get Business Cards

How many times have you been in a situation where someone wanted your contact information and you didn't have it right at hand? While we all love asking a bartender for a pen and a napkin, it's much easier when you have your business cards—even if you are unemployed.

Print up some simple ones on nice card stock at a local print shop or one of the Web sites listed below. They don't need to be fancy—they just need to include your name, phone number, and e-mail address. If you want, you can add something memorable, like "The Write Choice" or "Your Sales Solution." New contacts will respect your professionalism, and the cards give you something tangible to hand to new contacts. Check out these handy Web sites:

- www.vistaprint.com
- www.iprint.com

INTROVERT, SCHMINTROVERT!

Even the biggest social butterfly sometimes gets tired of having to make the effort to get to know new people.

But ultimately you have to begin "selling yourself" to strangers who may hold the key to your future. No matter how shy you are, this is something you definitely can do; after all, you've been in the working world a while now. You have accomplishments, goals you've achieved, products you've sold—you have good reason to be proud.

Need help getting started? Use e-mail to network with new people without having to approach them face to face. Or ask your friends to introduce you to people who can help you, and have them stay there with you to facilitate conversation—and brag about your strengths.

take a memo

Networking Tips

Before you head out to a meet-and-greet, keep these tips in mind:

- This is not a party. Yes, there may be food and even alcohol, but you are there first and foremost to find a job.
- Do your homework. Find out which organization is sponsoring the event, research the organization and any keynote speakers, and make a point of introducing yourself to them.
- Focus on the quality, not quantity, of your connections. You'll get better results from meeting the "right" people than from handing out business cards indiscriminately.
- Practice your pitch on people you trust to give you an honest assessment of how it plays.
- Make sure your presentation is impeccable. Dress appropriately for the event and take plenty of business cards and resumes.
- Be prepared to follow up after the event. Be sure to get contact information for any promising contacts you make.

Challenge yourself in small increments. Go to a party, a networking event, or a community event, and talk to one person for five minutes. Be sure to mention that you are looking for a job. At the very least you'll have met someone new who now has you in mind should a suitable job ever open up.

MAINTENANCE TIPS

Keeping up with your network doesn't mean it's all business all the time. It only takes a few moments to send out an e-mail congratulating a friend on his engagement or to make a phone call inquiring about a contact's new baby. (Don't worry, in a later conversation, you can remind her that you are still looking!)

Keep notes on your contacts' interests, birthdays, and life events. These will give you a legitimate reason to contact them from time to time, and give you something to discuss beyond "What can you do for me now?"

Set up reminders in your Yahoo! Calendar to send out e-mail blasts to your different groups (colleagues, family, alumni, and so on) to update them on your progress.

Don't Forget to Return the Favor

When you're well into your career, you're in a good position to help members of your network find jobs. You can introduce a contact to your manager, or pass along a resume to your human resources department. (Some companies even pay referral rewards to employees who find new employees!) So if you see a job that would interest someone in your network, or merely discover another good contact for someone, pass it on. Arrange a dinner so people in your network can meet one another.

This "golden rule" thinking will always have a good outcome, according to networking expert Diane Darling in her book *The Networking Survival Guide: Get the Success You Want by Tapping into the People You Know.* As she writes: "You have something to give everyone. It just takes a few questions to figure it out. If it's not immediately apparent, then stay connected to the quality of people you want in your life. Something good will come of it."

Quality versus Quantity

Remember that a bigger network is not necessarily a better network—you need to focus on quality contacts. As you expand your network, you'll begin to run across people who are insincere, don't return calls, or simply don't have time to follow through for you as they promised. Let these people go. Concentrate on those who can help you—and those you can help in return.

Don't Forget the Little People

Just as we tend to let our resume slide until we suddenly need it again, we sometimes let our network lapse after we find a job. As we get to know our new duties and coworkers, we understandably forget to stay connected.

But maintaining your network is a must! Sometimes even the best new jobs don't work out for reasons that may be out of your hands. While stocks go up and down and CEOs come and go, your job prospects will always remain solid if you regularly cultivate your network.

So stay in touch with your contacts—send occasional e-mails or cards to thank them and let them know how you're doing. Let them know about your major accomplishments. When you decide to change jobs again someday, you'll have a group of people waiting to help you reach the next rung up on your career ladder.

Recommended Books

The Networking Survival Guide: Get the Success You Want by Tapping into the People You Know by Diane Darling (McGraw-Hill, 2003, ISBN 0071409998, $14.95).

Never Eat Alone: And Other Secrets to Success, One Relationship at a Time by Keith Ferrazzi & Tahl Raz (Doubleday & Company, Inc., 2005, ISBN 0385512058, $24.95).

Dig Your Well Before You're Thirsty: The Only Networking Book You'll Ever Need by Harvey Mackay (Doubleday & Company, Inc., 1999, ISBN 0385485468, $15.95).

The Referral of a Lifetime: The Networking System that Produces Bottom-line Results . . . Every Day! (The Ken Blanchard Series) by Tim Templeton with Lynda Rutledge Stephenson (Berrett-Koehler Publishers, Inc., 2005, ISBN 1576753212, $14.95).

A Foot in the Door: Networking Your Way into the Hidden Job Market by Katharine Hansen (Ten Speed Press, 2000, ISBN 1580081401, $14.95).

How to Make People Like You in 90 Seconds or Less by Nicholas Boothman (Workman Publishing Company, Inc., 2000, ISBN 076111940X, $15.95).

How to Win Friends and Influence People by Dale Carnegie (Simon & Schuster, 1982, ISBN 0671723650, $7.99).

Recommended Web Sites

Yahoo! Groups:
http://groups.yahoo.com

Yahoo! Message Boards:
http://messages.yahoo.com

Yahoo! People Search:
http://people.yahoo.com

The Riley Guide's Networking Resource:
www.rileyguide.com/support.html

eHow—How to Make Small Talk:
www.ehow.com/how_10812_make-small-talk.html

The Shyness Homepage:
www.shyness.com

Weddles.com Association Directory:
www.weddles.com/associations

LinkedIn—Joins together people, jobs, and services:
www.linkedin.com

Jobster—Invitation-only network connecting employers with recommended professionals:
www.jobster.com

Friendster—Reach more than 20 million members online:
www.friendster.com

CHAPTER **5**

Web Wise: Starting Your Search Online

"First, they do an on-line search."

You may remember what job searching was like without the World Wide Web. Resumes had to be typewritten, and mistakes corrected with white paint. Job hunters' fingers became ink-stained as they scoured the Sunday paper's job classifieds. Job seekers would call anxiously about a job, only to wait endlessly on hold.

Fortunately, the Web has changed all that. Now the job seeker holds the cards. She can research everything about a company from the number of female executives to its recycling policies. She can learn all about a job's corporate culture, and discern keywords with which to fill her resume.

No matter what your level of familiarity with job searching online, we've got some resources—some you may have used, others not—that will make you an Internet job-seeking specialist in no time.

Enter the Internet

You probably use the Internet every day, and have conducted a job hunt or two (or ten) with it before. Even so, technology is always advancing. You may be unaware of just how many advantages the Web holds for your job hunt.

The Internet allows you to search and apply for jobs faster and more efficiently than ever before. Online you can find helpful information to research a company and prepare your resume and cover letter—and, of course, available jobs.

The best place to begin your search is with a **job board**. These Web sites not only offer jobs across every industry and all over the world but also give you control over how the jobs are sorted, organized, and stored. Other great sources for online job hunters are **company Web sites**, which are useful if you know the organization you want to work for. (But keep in mind that many companies do not keep their Web sites current; in addition, some do not show job listings at all or offer incomplete lists.)

Job Boards

Long gone are the days of typewritten resumes delivered by snail mail. Job boards have changed the entire landscape of job hunting. Sites like Yahoo! HotJobs and others offer one-stop-shopping for jobs on the Net (free of charge, too!).

On the following pages, we list the many benefits of searching and applying for positions using an online job board.

Specific Search Tools

Time is of the essence when you are searching for a job—especially if you are already employed or have a family. You need to save time any way you can.

Not to worry! Need a nursing job in Nebraska? A finance job with a Fortune 500 firm? Sites like Yahoo! HotJobs offer job seekers multiple search options to target exactly the kind of job they want: search by keyword, location, company, salary, experience level, employer type (direct employer or staffing agency), or when the job was posted. Better yet, you can save each search to run again whenever you choose.

E-mail Search Agents

An e-mail search agent is like your own personal assistant working 24/7 to retrieve jobs for you. Just enter the information you want the search agent to track down (heck, try using several agents!) and you'll be alerted by e-mail when matching jobs are posted.

Collected Job Listings

Recently Yahoo! HotJobs put its cutting-edge technology to work to "scrape" jobs from all over the Internet. In other words, no more searching dozens of sites to find the job you want: Instead, enter your search terms to select from a comprehensive collection of sites from across the Web.

Detailed Job Postings

If you've ever tried to decipher newspaper classifieds for a job search, you'll appreciate the wonderful invention of online job postings. They are a treasure trove of job information and tell you practically everything you need to know, short of the recruiter's home phone number!

Don't believe us? Here's proof. Take a look at a typical newspaper job ad:

NURSE, registered. F/T & p/T. Good sa-
lary & bfts, Anytown pvt hospice. Fax 555-****

Kind of like reading an eye chart, huh? Because newspaper job ads charge per word, job postings are seriously abbreviated.

Now take a look at an online job posting:

Hospice Nurse
Job ID: Hospice Nurse
Location: Anytown, USA
Date Posted: 01/22/2006

Hospice Nurse

Ever-Care Hospice is seeking a Patient Care Coordinator to oversee and direct all aspects of patient care for all home care patients under the care of Anytown Health and Human Services Department. The PCC will ensure the delivery of quality patient care through professional assessment, intervention, evaluation, and supervision of the entire patient team and plan of care.

Qualifications:

- Graduation from an approved school of nursing; current state registration.
- Minimum of three years of experience in medical-surgical, oncology or community health nursing or equivalent.
- Demonstrated ability to assist with and respond to the needs of patients and families in varied settings.
- Previous management experience.
- Prior hospice or home health experience.

Responsibilities:

- Ensure that all clinical services provided are consistent with the hospice standards of care and comply with all written policies and procedures in place for Ever-Care Hospice.
- Ensure that all clinical documentation is accurate and complies with all written policies and procedures and standards of practice for Ever-Care Hospice.
- Facilitate all home care visits, all documentation needed for recertification, etc.
- Participate in the QA Program.
- Maintain ongoing contact with physicians and other medical personnel.

Benefits:

- Company sponsors employee's medical insurance, short-term disability, $30,000 life insurance, and a great 401(k) plan with a company match of 50%.
- 24 paid time off days per year.
- Voluntary dental plans, supplementary and additional life insurance options available.

Apply to Job

Included here is everything you need to know about a job's requirements and expectations, such as "current state registration" and "previous management experience." You can also create a tailored resume and cover letter, including keywords like *hospice*, *oncology*, and *clinical services*, and get these materials to the right people.

Storing Your Stuff

Resumes, cover letters, phone numbers, e-mails, oh my! Who can keep up with all this stuff—especially when the baby is crying, the dog is chewing the sofa leg, and the tub is overflowing? Luckily, job boards are a convenient, free repository where you can store all your job search "junk." They can also help you track which jobs you applied for and when (no embarrassing, repetitive applications to the same job).

Community Commiseration

You're never alone in your job search—especially in cyberspace. Online message boards allow you to "meet" other job seekers (not to mention the occasional recruiter on the hunt for talent!) and get their input on jobs and companies. Just remember that some users may have a score to settle with a company that laid them off, so don't believe everything you read. Also, be wary of scam artists seeking your personal financial information. Don't disclose any personal information, like your bank account or Social Security numbers, and if a job sounds too good to be true (WORK FROM HOME!! MAKE $$!!), it probably is.

Research Resource

Experience aside, any job seeker who is armed with information stands ready to compete in the job market. Internet job boards offer A–Z facts and figures for just about anything you want to know.

- ☼ **Industry news feeds:** These give you the latest stories and trends in your area of interest—very helpful when you're writing a cover letter and need a solid statistic to throw in or when you're preparing for an interview and want to appear knowledgeable about recent industry developments.

- ☼ **E-mail newsletters:** These save you time by providing you with important information on industries like health care, technology, finance, and government without your having to hunt for it—the latest news, topical community posts and polls, as well as lists of companies that are currently hiring. (Sign up for Yahoo! HotJobs newsletters here: www.hotjobs.com/newsletters.)

☼ **Salary tools:** Perhaps the most important research of all you can conduct on a job site is salary research. Salary tools help you calculate
what you are "worth" in the marketplace—it's *imperative* to know this
before you go into an interview or a negotiation. You can also search
by region, so you'll know what to expect in salary from Pittsburgh to
Poughkeepsie.

Privacy

You don't want to post your job search information only to have your boss
present it to you the next day, nor do you want just any old employer to be able
to see it.

With job boards, you can choose to make your resume public, meaning
it will be searchable by the employers and staffing agencies that pay to use
the site. Conversely, you can keep it private, meaning your resume is not
searchable and can only be shared when you physically send it to a hiring
company.

In addition to these options, some sites give you the option of blocking certain employers from viewing your resume—regardless of whether the resume is
public or private. Yahoo! HotJobs pioneered this feature, which it calls "HotBlock."
You simply enter the names of the companies you do not want to be able to view
your resume and recruiters who identify themselves with that company will not be
shown your resume in their search results. It's an ideal way to help keep your current boss from finding out about your job search. Be cautious, however; there is
no way to keep company representatives from seeing your resume if they are
using a third party to recruit.

STRAIGHT FROM THE SOURCE: COMPANY WEB SITES

Realizing the power of the Web in finding top talent, companies themselves
have begun committing large portions of their own Web sites to job postings.
This saves the companies time and money by drawing in candidates directly,
rather than having recruiters fish for them. These company Web sites, too, are
free for you.

Company Web sites are particularly valuable for those who know the company where they would like to work. You can learn about the company's culture—
such as dress codes, communication style, and working hours. Most company
Web sites are upfront about their culture and benefits because they want to

attract employees who will make a good fit. By reading press releases, annual reports, and executive bios, you can get further insight into their mission, products, and services—and their expectations of employees.

Be aware, however, that you can only deduce so much about a company from its Web site—any scandals or big dips in stock value won't be readily available there, if at all. Be sure to use Yahoo! Finance and Yahoo! News to get a more objective report.

OTHER WEB RESOURCES

Here are some other Web sites you can use in your search:

A Career Crystal Ball

If you have a question about pretty much any job in the United States today, the Department of Labor and its *Occupational Outlook Handbook* (in book form or available for free on the Web, see "Recommended Web Sites" at the end of this chapter) will have information on it.

The OOH offers a wealth of information about everything from working conditions to required education to salary to statistics for more than 270 types of jobs. (Did you know, for instance, that most fashion designers are self-employed?) Revised every two years, it also projects what fields will grow or decline over the upcoming years. Use the OOH to get a basic idea of what your chosen fields would be like and to learn about the "downsides" from an objective resource. It also tells you about growing fields where jobs are becoming more plentiful.

Business Organization Web Sites

In chapter 4 we discussed networking face to face through business organizations. You should also visit these organizations' Web sites. They'll fill in the gaps for you on industries and jobs you might like but don't know enough about—and maybe have some of those jobs posted as well! They'll also list the latest news, statistics, and legislative activities for their members.

Also remember that there can be multiple sites for an industry—for example, the National Education Association (http://www.nea.org) covers teaching as a whole; the National Science Teachers Association (http://www.nsta.org) focuses on science teachers specifically. (See page 78 for examples of business organization Web sites.)

take a memo

A Sampling of Business Organization Sites:

American Bankers Association: http://www.aba.com

American Bar Association: http://www.abalawinfo.com

American Hospital Association: http://www.aha.org

American Insurance Association: http://www.aiadc.org

American Nurses Association: http://www.nursingworld.org

American Psychological Association: http://www.apa.org

Cellular Telecommunications Industry Association: http://www.ctia.org

Collegiate Sports Information Directors of America: http://www.cosida.com

International Game Development Association: http://www.igda.org

National Collegiate Athletics Association: http://www.ncaa.org

National Press Photographers Association: http://www.nppa.org

Snack Food Association: http://www.sfa.org/

Relocation Sites

Like salary calculators, relocation sites such as Yahoo! HotJobs Relocation and Homefair.com help you predict your living expenses at a new job in a new city. You can compare rental and ownership prices in any region of the country (sometimes foreign countries, too), and compare cost of living in two cities side by side. You can also calculate how much it would cost to hire trucks to move you, and investigate crime rates and school ratings.

For interest rates and other home financing information, your bank's Web site is a good starting point.

Minority Web Sites

Minority Web sites cater to segments of workers that historically have faced special challenges in finding competitive jobs. Sites such as the Hispanic Alliance for Career Enhancement (www.HACE-USA.org), the NAACP (www.naacp.org), and Career Women (www.careerwomen.com) help minorities find potential jobs and recognize their employment rights.

Other such sites include:

- ☼ Hirediversity.com
- ☼ LatPro.com
- ☼ WorkPlaceDiversity.com
- ☼ DiversityInc.com

Now that you have some ideas as to where and how to conduct your job search, let's explore what to do once you're ready to start applying for positions. In the upcoming chapters, we'll discuss how to craft job-winning cover letters and resumes, as well as how to handle the most challenging part of the job-hunting process—the interview.

Recommended Books

Targeting the Job You Want: For Job Hunters, Career Changers, Consultants and Freelancers, 3rd ed., by Kate Wendleton & Wendy Alfus Rothman (Thomson Delmar Learning, 2000, ISBN 1564144496, $19.99).

Occupational Outlook Handbook 2004–2005, U.S. Department of Labor (JIST Works, Inc., 2004, ISBN 1563709880, $16.90).

Everything Online Job Search Book: Find the Jobs, Send Your Resume and Land the Career of Your Dreams—All Online! by Steven Graber & Barry Littman (Adams Media Corporation, 2000, ISBN 1580623654, $12.95).

Guide to Internet Job Searching 2004–2005 by Margaret Riley Dikel & Frances E. Roehm (The McGraw-Hill Companies, 2004, ISBN 007141374X, $14.95).

Electronic Resumes and Online Networking: How to Use the Internet to Do a Better Job Search by Rebecca Smith (Career Press, Inc., 2000, ISBN 1564145115, $13.99).

Recommended Web Sites

Yahoo! HotJobs—Job Searching Tips:
http://hotjobs.yahoo.com/findingajob

Yahoo! HotJobs—Salary Wizard:
http://hotjobs.salary.com

Yahoo! HotJobs—Relocation:
http://hotjobs.yahoo.com/relocation

U.S. Department of Labor's Occupational Outlook Handbook:
www.bls.gov/oco

Internet Fraud Complaint Center:
www.ifccfbi.gov/index.asp

Better Business Bureau:
www.bbb.org

Weddles.com Tips for Success:
www.weddles.com/tips/seekers.htm

Homefair.com:
www.homefair.com

CHAPTER 6

The Cover Letter:
The Underutilized Advantage

"It's plotted out. I just have to write it."

It's the lament of many a midcareer job seeker: "*Why* do I have to write a cover letter?" Your resume sums you up, you're aware of what skills you possess and what you can offer—why do you have to restate it all in a cover letter?

Think of it this way: The resume is formal and straightforward, with little room for any flavor. But a cover letter gives you a chance, in real sentences instead of only bullet points, to talk to the recruiter as a regular person, and show him that you are a seasoned, serious job seeker who can really help his company.

In flowing or snappy prose (depending on your writing style), you can relate your experience to the company's needs. You can emphasize your interest in working there, any special circumstances that make you a stronger candidate than others for the job, and other compelling details.

Most important, the cover letter *succinctly* highlights your top skills and accomplishments—and makes the reader want to learn more about you by reading your resume.

MORE THAN AN INTRODUCTION

Even veteran job seekers make the mistake of using the cover letter as little more than a "Hello, My Name Is" sticker at a trade show, making only a brief mention of your name and the job for which you are applying, and leaving your resume to fill in the blanks.

However, your cover letter is a valuable opportunity. First, it's your chance to demonstrate in just a few sentences how well you understand what the company needs in filling this job (and why that's you!). It's also a tool to explain any lapses in your professional background if you are changing fields or have a disjointed career path, rather than trying to tackle or ignore these issues on a resume. (We'll talk about these and other trouble spots later in the chapter.)

Finally, the cover letter allows you to illustrate how well you match up with the job being advertised by drawing direct parallels between your experience and the job requirements. This effort alone will put you well ahead of many of the other candidates.

So before you start writing, first make some notes—you want to customize your letter as much as possible, not just bang out a form letter. Recruiters will spot that a mile away. You need to find the key matches between the job requirements and your skills, and highlight each one.

Read over the job description carefully several times. Ask yourself: *What does the job description specify as the primary responsibilities? What keywords stand out?* Then create a list of your own skills and experience, and figure out how they

take a memo

Electronic versus Paper Cover Letters

In today's electronic age, you will likely be sending out more e-mail cover letters than paper ones. Because we use e-mail so much, and because recruiters prefer e-mail (a whopping 83 percent of recruiters surveyed by Yahoo! HotJobs prefer receiving resumes via e-mail), it's easy to be a little lax in writing your electronic cover letter.

But you should be just as careful when writing an e-mail cover letter as you would writing a paper cover letter. Here are some tips:

- ☼ Follow traditional business letter etiquette, even though you're sending your letter electronically.

- ☼ Include all your contact information, including your e-mail address and mobile phone number.

- ☼ Attach your resume and work samples, if requested. If you are linking to work samples, double-check the hyperlinks.

- ☼ We can all forget this one simple step: Use spell-check, and then check all the spelling again yourself. You'd hate to claim that your attention to detail makes you a perfect fit for "there company."

parallel the job's requirements. (This will also help when it's time to tailor your resume to the job.)

You may find that you have a lot to include in your cover letter, but it's important to focus on only the strongest points, since, as a rule, the letter should be no longer than one page. However, keep in mind that in certain industries—and for positions at certain levels of management—hiring managers do not frown on a succinct cover letter that's longer than a page. Be sure to do your research into this beforehand.

GET IT WRITE

A cover letter is a simple thing—yet it requires attention to do it well.

The body of a cover letter can be broken down into three basic parts:

- ☼ **Opening (1–2 paragraphs):** Here is where you introduce yourself, state the job you are applying for, and specify why it interests you. Be sure you *include the job title* as it is listed in the job advertisement, along with any identifying codes.

☼ **What You Can Do for Them (1–2 paragraphs):** Here you explain what you have to offer, not what the company can do for you. Using the job advertisement as your guide, specify your skills and accomplishments— the ones that match those being sought by the employer. Do not rehash your entire resume. Remember, most hiring decisions come down to three things: Can you do the job? Will you do the job? And will you fit in? These are all questions you should try to answer in the body of the cover letter.

☼ **Why You Should Work Together (1 paragraph):** Summarize why you would make a great addition to their team and point out that you have more information to back up that claim. Include a time when you will call to follow up.

Of course, you'll also need an inside address (recruiter's name and title, company, and address), a salutation (Dear Ms. Johnson), and the conclusion ("Sincerely, Mike Smith"). If you are sending the letter via fax, "snail mail," or as an attachment to an e-mail, you'll want to include your address and that of the company, just as you would with any business letter. However, if you are sending the cover letter in the body of an e-mail, you may opt simply to begin with the salutation.

Be sure to address a particular person, not "To Whom It May Concern." Get a name either from the job ad, the company Web site, or even by calling the company and asking for a recruiter in the human resources department. If you absolutely cannot find a name, then address the letter to "Dear Recruiter" or "Dear Human Resources Director." Never say "Dear Sir" or "Dear Madam"—you don't know whether it will be a man or a woman who ultimately reads your letter.

take a memo

Who's Who?

Honorifics like *Mr.* and *Mrs.* are preferred by some, but not by others. Be sensitive to this. It's also important to realize that some people might have professional honorifics, like *Dr.*, and prefer to be addressed as such.

If you are addressing a woman, simply use *Ms.*

If you cannot figure out whether the recruiter's name belongs to a man or a woman (as in "Kris," "Pat," or "Joe/Jo"), call the company and ask how to properly address the recruiter. Finally, unless asked, do not address a person you don't know by first name—this may jeopardize your relationship with them right off the bat.

Section One: Open Wide

Journalists are taught to begin every article with a strong lead paragraph—
a punchy, sharp opening that immediately draws the reader in and keeps her
reading. The same applies to your cover letter. For your first sentence you want
a strong opening—*not* "My name is . . . " (that's already noted in several places)
or "I'm applying for XYZ job."

Yes, you need to state the job for which you are applying, and the sooner the
better—a recruiter shouldn't have to read your entire letter to figure out what job
you're applying for. Just do so in a catchy way:

> *Dear Mr. Wright,*
>
> *Clients come for the services; they stay for the relationships. I would
> like to develop strong client relationships as the next Account
> Executive for Acme, Inc., per your job ad # X47KD as listed on Yahoo!
> HotJobs.*

The lead-off paragraph needs to grab the recruiter's attention and make a
strong statement about you. Here are some approaches you can use:

Referral: Remember that great network you've been building? Now's your
chance to use it:

> *Dear Ms. Wadsworth,*
>
> *Your regional vice president, Tom Jackson, suggested that I contact
> you because, with my background in teaching, he thought I'd be an
> asset as a trainer in your human resources department.*

(This opening mentions a human being's name and relates company business
to your experience and interests.)

Success Record: Here you start off with strong proof of your past success.
Mention concrete numbers if possible:

> *Dear Mr. Samuels,*
>
> *As manager of new business development for Office Supplies
> Worldwide, I exceeded the annual sales goals by 19 percent, securing
> six new clients and boosting profits by nearly $500,000.*

(This mentions hard numbers, a leadership position, and a brand name.)

General Knowledge: Demonstrate a broad understanding of your field:

Dear Ms. Johnson,

Home and garden television shows have grown more than 20 percent during the last five years. With ten years of marketing and television production experience, I believe I can capitalize on this trend as The Home Place's new Director of Marketing.

(This shows you are on top of the trends.)

News-related: Mention a recent article or television piece about the company:

Dear Mr. Evans,

The May 24 New York Times *article about Acme's new line of rust-proof tools intrigued me. As an account executive, I have sold rust-proof grills for Grill King for three years and would like to apply my knowledge in a sales position in the home improvement industry.*

(This gives the date the article appeared and the publication name, and relates the company's business to your experience.)

SECTION TWO: WHY YOU ARE GREAT FOR THE JOB

This is your opportunity to talk about some of your qualifications and how they work in the context of the job for which you're applying. A few things to remember:

Keep your sentences clear and brief. According to SHRM, recruiters spend an average of sixty seconds or less reading cover letters—don't give them a reason to spend any less time on yours.

Refer to, but don't rehash, your resume. Rather, select your two or three most impressive accomplishments that relate to the job for which you are applying. You can always discuss other accomplishments in an interview.

If you're applying for a job you found in an ad, **be sure to refer to the ad's requirements here**. If the ad asks for Microsoft Excel, and you are skilled in it, say so. If the ad requires proven experience in leading a team, or Java, or Mandarin Chinese, specify your accomplishments in those areas as well. Mention the skills by name—even quote the job ad word for word if you have to. However . . .

Keep jargon and flowery language to a minimum. Although you should include keywords directly from the ad, chances are the recruiter is a generalist.

He is not going to know what every acronym means. Be very clear about your skills and your experience: If the ad specifies that a "J.D." is required, it's OK to use that abbreviation in your cover letter; otherwise use "law degree." If you were the director of personnel, use that title or a similar phrase as opposed to Vice President of People. Avoid stilted language, like the following: "It is my most sincere hope that you will consider me for employment with your esteemed organization." This kind of over-the-top phrasing is a big turn-off. Don't use it.

Now let's see what the body of your letter looks like when you keep these points in mind. Perhaps you're applying for an account executive position with a public relations firm. The firm seeks a "self-starter" with "first-rate communication skills" and an "understanding of the health care industry." You might write:

As assistant public relations director for Heart and Hands Hospice in Bloomington, Indiana, I developed a thorough understanding of the health care industry and the challenges of caring for aging consumers as costs kept rising. I relied on my communication skills daily to promote the hospice's brand and solicit funds from public and private donors. A determined self-starter, I exceeded department fund-raising goals by 17 percent despite limited support staff budget cuts.

Note how this person uses keywords taken directly from the job posting, and gives a summary of his accomplishments without getting too detailed—save that for the resume and the interview. He also offers a hard number (17 percent) that immediately makes the recruiter want to find out what other successes lie within the resume.

Or consider this cover letter body for a lawyer applying for a corporate counsel position requiring "five to seven years' experience," "familiarity with intellectual property issues," and "initiative and sound judgment":

Of particular note as you consider hiring the next member of your team are my seven years' experience at Wesson and Eads International, a leading global software firm. There, as assistant director of the Internet and E-Commerce Law Department, I drew on my training in intellectual property issues, initiative, and sound judgment to handle several major initiatives:

- *Patented OfficeDeskPro 2.0, (software you may well use on your own computers), which grossed $12.3 million in sales in 2005*
- *Drafted and negotiated commercial contracts*
- *Served as liaison to U.S. Patent and Trade Office*

Note that this person uses (limited) bullet points to offer highlights of her career while also using keywords from the ad.

You may think you need more than one to two paragraphs to describe your worthiness for the job—that your considerable experience and education belong in the cover letter. Confine yourself to accomplishments that *relate to the job*. Too often people think that listing everything notable in their background will land them the job. But make a cover letter too long, and no one will want to read the accompanying resume (which is the real point of the cover letter, after all).

So, use your best judgment, stick to the two to three highlights that most relate to the job, and keep the letter succinct.

Section Three: Working Together

Your final paragraph should fuse your skills and the company's needs—showing how you could work well together to make the company more successful. For example, for a Web designer seeking a position with a creative services firm:

> *I believe my experience in designing Web pages for the nonprofit industry would benefit the clients you represent, such as G.I.V.E. and The Food Pantry. My familiarity with user interface studies and graphic design can help Power Pages Creative Services not only continue to satisfy your current client base, but also bring in new business.*

Be sure to offer to contact the recruiter within the next week to follow up. Give your contact information should she want to speak to you in the meantime:

> *I would appreciate an opportunity to meet with you to discuss this position. I will call you next Monday, August 25, to follow up. In the meantime, you can reach me at (555) 555-5555.*
> *Sincerely,*
> *Bob Jacobs*

Sometimes a job ad won't give a phone number or will specifically state, "No phone calls." Recruiters do this to manage their time and avoid being inundated by calls from job seekers.

It's best to approach such a recruiter with caution. Consider following up first via e-mail. Explain that you simply want to be sure he received your resume. (Even if the ad does not give an e-mail address, you can usually find the HR department e-mail address by visiting the company Web site.) If an e-mail fails to elicit a response, feel free to call the company switchboard (also listed on the Web site) and ask for the human resources department. State who you are and the job for which you have applied, and ask if there is anything else the recruiter needs from you. Be brief and polite—no one can fault you for following up.

OTHER TROUBLESOME TOPICS

Cover letters pose some particular stumbling blocks for midcareer professionals. Let's take a look at how to handle them.

Summing Yourself Up

As with resumes, much of the difficulty in writing cover letters can lie in knowing exactly what to put in them—especially if you have extensive experience. Again, always focus on what the job posting asks for, and tailor your letter appropriately.

But what if you are changing fields altogether, say, moving from teaching into sales? How do you address this in a cover letter, if at all?

You still want to focus on your key skills—get right to the point of how your teaching experience will make you a good salesperson. For example, you could open with a statement like this:

I believe that if you can successfully sell American history to eighth graders, you can sell anything—including microprocessors.

You can then go on to explain how your background in technology (using computers for research), writing and public speaking (preparing and delivering lectures), budgeting (planning field trips), leadership (coaching the softball team), and motivation (implementing reward systems for students' work) can all be applied to the sales field. Ultimately, there's a reason you're interested in this new career and a reason you think you'd be good at it. Find these reasons and highlight them.

Layoffs/Job Changes

Another obstacle you may face is a background of layoffs and other job changes—do you mention these in the cover letter?

The answer is no, not directly. You have your resume and interview to explain any perceived gaps. Because the cover letter is the very first message about you the recruiter will see, you want it to be as positive as possible. So instead, sum up your many experiences so that the emphasis is on the skills you've gained, not the path you've taken to get there:

☼ *With ten years' experience as a registered nurse . . .* (Due to cutbacks and two pregnancies, this candidate has actually worked at four different hospitals in those ten years.)

☼ *My skills include recruiting, training, and employee development across companies of all sizes* . . . (This applicant worked in human resources for several dot-coms that folded, before contracting with a larger company.)

☼ *I've contributed travel, business, and fashion articles to national publications such as* The Journal, The Daily Ledger, *and* Global News Weekly . . . (This writer has had stints both as a staff reporter and as a freelancer for many different publications.)

Salary/Reference Requirements

Generally, you do not need to include salary requirements and references in your cover letter.

The cover letter should be as brief and succinct as possible—references simply don't belong there, except for perhaps mentioning the person who referred you to the job. Otherwise, you can give the recruiter a list of your references at a later date.

Salary requirements, however, will need to come up at some point—preferably during the interview. It's best to leave them out of the cover letter because, again, the cover letter is the first message about you the recruiter will see. You don't want her eyes immediately drawn to your compensation demands.

However, if the job ad states adamantly that salary requirements are a must, you can include them in the cover letter, toward the end. Be sure to list a range, not a hard number, since you want to leave room for some flexibility. (We'll discuss salary further in chapters 9 and 10.)

THE FINAL PRODUCT

Now that you understand the components of and the right approach to take in a cover letter, let's put it all together.

Let's say you are seeking a position developing campaigns for an advertising firm. You have an undergraduate degree in English, and have worked the last five years in various public relations and communications jobs for a pharmaceutical company. On weekends you teach creative writing classes at a youth center.

You spot a job posting on Yahoo! HotJobs for a copywriter position at a large advertising firm. The firm seeks someone who is deadline-oriented, creative, and has fresh ideas and strong writing skills. The applicant must also be able to edit copy and have a familiarity with medical terminology.

take a memo

Don't Become a Cover Letter Statistic

A badly written cover letter can hurt your chances. More than 76 percent of recruiters said in a recent SHRM survey that they would not consider a cover letter with typos, or at best they would toss the accompanying resume into a file rather than consider it for that current job.

The most common cover letter blunders are the following:

Name That Job: Recruiters often try to fill more than one job simultaneously. After the salutation, state exactly which job you're applying for.

Form Letters: The point of a cover letter is to make a personal connection with the reader. Tailor your letter specifically to each company you send it to.

Don't Repeat Yourself: Don't regurgitate everything that's in your resume—offer deeper insights into what your resume does *not* say. Provide an in-depth explanation of some of your key achievements at your last job, for instance, and how those accomplishments could help the company. Or tell a story about a tough problem you solved.

What's in It for Me?: Don't say you are applying for the job because of the money, the travel opportunities, a better commute, or anything else that concerns only you.

Balance Confidence and Humility: While you certainly want to appear competent, arrogance can turn a recruiter off: "Throw away all those other resumes—I'm your guy!" Show enthusiasm and a positive attitude, but don't overdo it.

First you highlight the important skills the job requires: "deadline-oriented," "creative," and so on.

As you draw parallels between your experience and the job requirements, you note that both your marketing jobs and your volunteer work require many if not all the required skills. In addition, working for a pharmaceutical company has given you an insider's look at the health care industry.

You already have the skills this job seeks, and more—now you just need to present your background properly.

On the next page, you'll find an example of a cover letter that effectively addresses this job's requirements.

John Smith
123 Stephens Street
Anytown, USA 12345

Ella Dowling, Human Resources Director
Awesome Ads, Inc.
100 Main Street
Anytown, USA 55555

July 30, 2005

Dear Ms. Dowling:

I was struck by the story in the July 22 *Anytown Times* that Awesome Ads, Inc., is expanding its business into the health care industry. **[Opens with strong knowledge of the company and a reference to a recent news story]** I believe my experience both in pharmaceutical marketing and creative writing makes me a unique match for the Copywriter position, #XC77Y on Yahoo! HotJobs. **[States job title, number, and exactly why he is qualified to apply]**

As a public relations manager for PharmCorp International, I:

- Developed my creativity and writing skills in deadline-oriented environments.
- Gained a strong understanding of medical terminology and concepts, particularly as they're applied to pharmaceuticals.
- Contributed fresh ideas for consumer outreach in times of rising health care costs and public distrust of pharmaceutical companies.

[Mentions skills from the ad verbatim and demonstrates knowledge of the medical/ pharmaceutical field]

In addition, volunteering with the Anytown Heads-Up literacy program has equipped me with the ability to make words exciting and foreign concepts understandable to a broad audience. **[Not mentioned in the ad but important to copywriting]** I also have a number of contacts in the pharmaceutical industry who often seek outside creative services for their advertising and marketing efforts. **[Offers the possibility of new business]**

I would appreciate an opportunity to meet with you to discuss the Copywriter position. I will call you next Monday, August 8, to follow up. In the meantime, you can reach me at 555-5555. **[States follow-up information and date]**

Sincerely,
John Smith

COVER LETTER CHEAT SHEET

We've already mentioned some style points to keep in mind, but they are important enough to bear repeating:

- ☼ Don't open with "To Whom It May Concern"—get a name.
- ☼ Highlight first and foremost your skills and experiences that match those the employer is seeking.
- ☼ Open with a strong lead sentence.
- ☼ Refer to the job ad and its specific language.
- ☼ Offer to follow up with the recruiter—and do it!
- ☼ For electronic letters, attach your resume and make sure any links to work samples you include work.
- ☼ Proofread your work.

Now for a few more:

- ☼ Use power words like "led," "leveraged," "initiated," and "created." Also use active voice. That is, rather than "The division's profits were raised 10 percent," say: "I raised the division's profits by 10 percent."
- ☼ Make sure your language is neither stiff nor too informal.
- ☼ Don't call the recruiter by first name, even if you have met before.
- ☼ When touting your achievements, be confident but don't exaggerate or lie.

Before You Hit *Send*

Some parting thoughts before you send that letter off into cyberspace:

Proofread and spell-check your letter. Now do it again. Ask a friend or family member to read your cover letter for typos and grammatical errors. If you're stuck on a grammatical point, consult a guide such as the classic *Elements of Style* by William Strunk Jr. and E. B. White or the *Chicago Manual of Style*.

Finally, send the letter to yourself as a test to check formatting. If you find errors, correct them and read it one more time—it's easy to overlook a mistake, and you don't want a typo ruining all your hard work.

A cover letter may be a brief document, but it's an important one. It introduces you to the recruiter and interests him or her in reading another important document—your resume. In chapter 7, we'll look at how to put together your experience and skills in a winning resume.

Recommended Books

Writing a Résumé and Cover Letter (Barnes & Noble Basics Series) by Susan Stellin (Silver Lining Books, 2003, ISBN 0760737924, $9.95).

Get the Interview Every Time: Fortune 500 Hiring Professionals' Tips for Writing Winning Résumés and Cover Letters by Brenda Greene (Dearborn, 2004, ISBN 0793183022, $12.95).

Cover Letters for Dummies by Joyce Lain Kennedy (John Wiley & Sons, Inc., 2000, ISBN 0764552244, $16.99).

Gallery of Best Cover Letters: A Collection of Quality Cover Letters by Professional Resume Writers by David F. Noble (JIST Works, Inc., 2004, ISBN 1563709902, $18.95).

The Elements of Style by William Strunk Jr. & E. B. White (Pearson Education, 1999, ISBN 020530902X, $7.95).

Recommended Web Sites

Yahoo/HotJobs—Resume and Cover Letters Tools:
http://hotjobs.yahoo.com/resume

Riley Guide—Cover Letters and Other Correspondence:
www.rileyguide.com/cover.html

George Mason University's Job Search Letters:
http://careers.gmu.edu/students/jobhunt/letters.html

University of California at Berkeley's Boring Cover Letters:
http://career.berkeley.edu/Article/030912a.stm

CHAPTER 7

Your Calling Card:
Crafting Your Resume

*"I'd like to keep a copy of your résumé on file.
Every now and then I need a good laugh."*

If you need a self-esteem boost, try reading your resume—all those skills, promotions, and rewards together on one page.

Writing a resume, on the other hand, can be a big, fat pain in the laptop— especially for midcareer professionals. When you first started your career, you had to use a fourteen-point font to describe your "culinary service skills" (waiting tables) or come up with a creative way to cite your award for winning the sorority sing-along. Now, as a midcareer job seeker, you have some real-world experience under your belt.

And that can actually be a big problem—especially if your experience straddles several different types of jobs (for example, your path from executive assistant to sales to public relations). By now you might have enough of a background for a ream of resumes—and too many job seekers want to cram every bit of it in. As you hone your career path to jobs that truly fit you, you have to figure out exactly what to put on the resume—and (sometimes more important) what to leave off.

A bigger issue, however, is that even after years in the workforce, many job seekers *still* don't know how to write a resume.

We can understand the frustration. No matter what your age or experience, there are some resume questions that universally plague job seekers. Certain classics never go away: *How long should it be? What if I've been out of the workforce raising my family? What if I was fired?*

Fear not: We have some ingenious solutions for you. In this chapter we'll show you how to craft a winning resume by customizing it to the particular job you are applying for. We'll also show you how to organize it, playing up your strengths and downplaying your weaknesses—and tackle some of the more challenging resume dilemmas you're likely to encounter.

WHAT DO I INCLUDE?

Leo Tolstoy's *War and Peace* is considered one of the greatest novels ever written. But there's a reason you don't see people carrying it on the subway: It's just too long!

Recruiters recoil when they pick up resumes packed with endless, eye-numbing text. As we've stated before, recruiters are screening for a number of jobs simultaneously and have limited time. You may have years of great experience and skills, but not all of those accomplishments belong on your resume— nor does a recruiter want to see them. Generally speaking, he is only interested in the skills you have that match those the hiring manager is seeking.

For example, let's say you're a computer programmer seeking to become a company's director of technology. You want your resume to demonstrate your technology and leadership skills and your most recent successes—not your six-month stint as a dog food salesman eight years ago.

(Unless, of course, you were named "Dog Food Salesman of the Year." If you have particularly stellar accomplishments that set you apart from the rest of the, umm, pack—major awards, offices held, advanced schooling, etc.—then you'll want to include on your resume the position where you achieved that recognition, even if it is unrelated to the job you are currently pursuing. We'll discuss that further on pages 108–109.)

hot facts

How Many Pages?

Yes, your resume can be more than one page—within reason. A HotJobs survey of recruiters found that more than 53 percent of respondents said it was acceptable for a resume to be longer than one page; 41 percent said it was acceptable only if the applicant had extensive experience; and 6 percent said it was not acceptable. So write away—just make sure:

☼ Your resume is *no longer* than two pages (although for executives and certain fields, such as science and academia, a longer resume is acceptable, usually in the form of a curriculum vitae, or CV).

☼ The experiences you list are *relevant to the job*.

CUSTOMIZING YOUR RESUME

Just as you tailor a cover letter to a job, you must do the same with your resume. Why? Because resumes aren't one-size-fits-all. Different companies have different expectations and definitions for different jobs. You don't want to blast out the exact same resume for all the sales jobs that interest you—selling pharmaceuticals requires a different skill set from selling real estate.

The good news is that many other job seekers *are* sending out the same resume to everyone. Just as with cover letters, you will stand out by making the effort to customize your resume.

How do you do this?

Prioritize the Particulars

Customizing your resume doesn't mean you have to completely rewrite one every time you apply for a job—it just means you need to prioritize the particular qualities a job requires.

So, carefully read through the job description, and pay attention to the details. Don't think, "How can I get across all my fantastic skills?" but rather, "What is this company looking for, and what in my work history will best demonstrate that I have what they need?"

To determine this, ask yourself the following questions: What keywords and skills are emphasized? What finer points stand out? In other words, you may be looking for *writing* jobs, but does the job description seem to require more *writing* or *editing* (a related skill)? Is the writing more *creative* or *technical* in nature? These are small, semantic differences, but major skills differences for you.

Understand these differences, and you can better tailor your resume to the job—saving time both for the recruiter and for yourself, and avoiding applying for jobs you don't want.

What's Relevant?

Next, put aside the job posting for a moment and list your past jobs, their biggest tasks, and your resulting strengths and accomplishments. Use numbers wherever you can ("No. 1 rep in the Southeast"; "Reduced turnover by 18%").

Now note which of these accomplishments best fit the job posting—these are jobs and skills you'll want to highlight in detail on your resume.

For example, if the posting asks for a "proven sales leader with the power to motivate others," then you'll want to discuss (prominently) on the resume the 23% increase in your team's sales at Job X, the $500,000 new account you landed, and your 91% employee satisfaction rate. You'll also want to list how you accomplished these things, such as through incentive programs or an open-door policy in which employees could easily approach you. Don't be afraid to toot your own horn (as long as what you write is related to the job you are seeking).

If you're applying for a graphic design job, should you mention your two years as a project manager at High-Flyers Airlines? Use your best judgment here. If you find parallels between your project manager experience—timeliness, attention to detail, software training, and other hard and soft skills—that apply to the job you're seeking, then by all means, list the relevant accomplishments of that job. And remember, you always have the cover letter and interview to mention what doesn't fit on the resume.

Winning at the Numbers Game

Not every professional accomplishment is easy to convey in numbers. Creative professionals, for example, like writers and artists, rarely have to meet sales goals, and their contributions to revenue enhancement are usually more indirect.

The key for these professionals is to find ways to demonstrate the importance of their contributions in other ways. For example, a graphic designer may have designed a new company logo just in time for a trade show the following day; an executive assistant may have contributed to meeting a department manager's goal of coming in 10 percent under budget by exercising creative cost-cutting in everyday tasks.

Also, use powerful phrases to describe your work—"spearheaded a team," "galvanized my staff."

Point out the more subtle ways your work helped a company meet a goal or respond in a crisis—this work is just as important as meeting sales quotas yourself.

FINDING A FORMAT

The seemingly simple Rubik's Cube caused quite a sensation in the early '80s. The colorful cubic puzzle frustrated millions, many of whom probably struggled with it for a few minutes, then gave up and tossed it aside for something easier to deal with like a Pet Rock or a Cabbage Patch Kid.

It is much the same with resumes. Like the crazy colors of a Rubik's Cube, resumes with too much clutter or bad organization will get tossed aside for ones that are easier to read.

Resume formatting can be understandably confusing, even for people who've been in the workforce for years. Every industry seems to have its own preferences, and for every rule there is an exception.

But here's the good news: Resumes have several standard formats that recruiters prefer and expect from midcareer job seekers. And you can take comfort in these limitations—there's no need to get creative or master advanced desktop publishing skills. With resumes, the simpler the better.

You are probably familiar with what a resume looks like, but let's do a quick review of the two basic resume formats that best apply to midcareer job seekers: chronological and functional.

hot facts ●●

Time Is Not on Your Side

The majority of recruiters spend less than three minutes reviewing a resume, according to a survey conducted by the Society for Human Resource Management. The easier you make it for them, the better chance you'll have of them reading your resume.

Chronological Format

Chronological format (sometimes called "reverse chronological" format) is the most popular way to construct a resume. It lists your work experience from most to least recent and provides dates and descriptions of each job. Recruiters prefer this format—84 percent said so in a Yahoo! HotJobs survey. (For an example of a resume that follows this format, see page 114, later in this chapter.)

Functional Format

Functional resumes are more ability-focused. These resumes are geared toward what the specific job requires and what the job seeker can do for the company, rather than detailing a linear work history. They are best used by those who have had disjointed employment histories—firings, leaving the workforce to raise a family, or other scenarios such as:

- ☼ You have a mixed work history, with no obvious connections between the jobs you've held.
- ☼ Your job titles, such as "Project Director" or "Account Manager," do not clearly reflect the scope and level of your skills.
- ☼ You are making a career change—either changing within your industry (from nursing to pharmaceutical sales) or changing your occupation (from nurse to writer).

Those who have had many similar jobs can also benefit from this format by consolidating experiences rather than listing every job.

The functional resume helps you clarify your work history and demonstrate skills and accomplishments that might not be obvious to the employer in a traditional chronological format. (For an example of a resume that follows this format, see page 116, later in this chapter.)

Sometimes a functional resume can be a red flag to a recruiter that an applicant may have something to hide about her work history, so use it wisely.

WEB-READY RESUMES

As you search online job sites, you'll be submitting various versions of your resume. You can submit your resume in several ways, depending on the site:

- ☼ Create a resume by filling in set fields.
- ☼ Cut and paste the resume from a document.
- ☼ Upload it directly to the site's database from your computer.

Note that when you cut and paste, you'll need to use ASCII (American Standard Code for Information Exchange), a universal character set that any computer can read (also known as "plain text"). Here's a tip: You'll want to save a copy of your ASCII resume both with the job site and on your own hard drive—so when you need to enter the resume into another Web site, you'll already have an ASCII copy to cut and paste. As always, before submitting a copy of your resume, make sure that you've tailored it to the specific job posting.

Functional resume users will want to upload their resume directly from their hard drive, if at all possible, since standard resume databases work chronologically.

BASIC ARRANGEMENT OF A CHRONOLOGICAL RESUME

A chronological resume follows a basic pattern:

- ☼ Contact Information
- ☼ Objective Statement, Summary Statement, or Summary of Qualifications
- ☼ Experience from most to least recent
- ☼ Awards and Honors
- ☼ Skills
- ☼ Education
- ☼ Volunteer Work and Activities

This is merely a guideline; it's not etched in stone. Depending on their relevance to the job, you may want to move some of these sections higher up. Bottom line: Whatever you feel is most important to the employer—list that first.

take a memo

Plain Text Tips

While plain text resumes may seem boring, their simplicity allows recruiters to view them the same way regardless of the software they use.

Creating the resume: If you're writing the resume from scratch, keep the organization clean and simple. Use plain text tools like Notepad or Wordpad. If you cut and paste a formatted resume, you'll notice that much of the formatting will be lost. Your font will be uniform and any text with bold or italics will be replaced with plain text. Save the resume as a text document (with a ".txt" extension).

Spell-check: A text editor likely won't have a spell-check function, so perform that in your word processing program, and then resave the updated plain text resume in the text editor.

E-mail: If you are asked to submit a resume pasted directly into an e-mail, some e-mail programs will add formatting you don't want. Double-check your characters and spacing, and be sure your e-mail program's features, such as "Rich Text Editor," are turned off.

Formatting: Use all CAPS to make headers stand out from body text. Use asterisks or dashes as "bullets." Avoid the "Tab" key; use the space bar instead. Finally, e-mail a copy of your plain-text resume to yourself before sending it to a recruiter, so you can see the resume as he will see it.

CONTACT INFORMATION

This is, of course, your name, home address, phone number, and e-mail address. Be especially careful about your e-mail address: If your e-mail identity is "GoRedSox" or "RollinsFamily," you need to create a more formal e-mail account just for job searching. When listing a phone number, use a home or cell number on which you can speak freely (not your current work number).

OBJECTIVE STATEMENTS

The objective or summary statement consists of one or two sentences at the beginning of your resume briefly summarizing the type of job you're seeking, your qualifications, or both.

There are several approaches to objective statements: **standard objective statements**, **summary statements**, and the **summary of qualifications**.

Standard Objective Statements

There has been some debate over whether or not to list an objective statement. On the "pro" side, it helps the job seeker target a specific position, and demonstrates that you know what you want professionally. It also tells the recruiter right away what type of job a candidate will fit and what skills the recruiter has to work with.

On the "con" side, some feel an objective statement limits you to just one position when you might be qualified for others. However, if you make the statement broad enough and keep the *company's* needs in mind, as opposed to your own, you'll be fine. We feel it's always good to lead off with your objective.

The standard objective statement works well both for those who are certain of what job they want to pursue, and those whose career goals are not as clear. It should be simple, specific, and brief, and should highlight what skills and experience you have to offer the company. Examples include:

- ☼ A position in which I can draw on my eight years of experience as an intellectual property attorney to help bring ABC Fixtures' exciting new products to the public ahead of the competition.

Or,

- ☼ To use my sales and marketing experience to boost nonprofits' donations and public exposure.

Do *not* use the following:

- ☼ To make money doing . . .
- ☼ To find a stepping-stone to . . .
- ☼ A position that allows me a flexible schedule for my kids . . .

These things may be what you want and deserve, but the resume is not the place to state them. As we've said, you need to keep in mind what the company needs, not your own needs.

Review your objective each time you send out a resume and make sure it fits the job you're applying for. Just as you should have several versions of your resume, you should also have several versions of your job objective—and an objective that actually names the company will demonstrate your attention to detail and your focus on what the company requires. (Just be sure to edit it before you send your resume to another company!)

Summary Statements

If you're less sure of your career goals, another approach is the summary statement. While an objective statement is a brief overview that focuses on what you seek from a specific job in the *future*, a summary statement sums up in a few sentences a job seeker's abilities and her accomplishments in the *past*. It highlights what makes you a qualified candidate as well as what makes you different from (and better than) other applicants.

As always, tailor your summary statement to highlight the experience that is most relevant to the job you're applying for. Here's an example of a strong summary statement:

Summary Statement: *Motivated senior leader and IT professional with experience in all aspects of Web application development and Linux servers. Award-winning manager. Possess in-depth understanding of emerging technologies and their ability to increase productivity, streamline production, and enhance overall company performance.*

Summary of Qualifications

Sometimes a job objective is too targeted and a summary statement is too short to highlight all your accomplishments. However, you have another choice: the summary of qualifications. A summary of qualifications is a brief list of your significant career accomplishments, highlighting the most important, relevant parts of a long, detailed resume. It's ideal for job seekers who have a long work history or who are applying for more senior positions.

A summary of qualifications differs from a summary statement in two key ways:

1. It's formatted as a list of items rather than a single statement, and
2. It highlights specific accomplishments rather than general achievements.

This section also goes by many names, including "Key Accomplishments" and "Career Highlights."

For maximum effectiveness, the list should include no more than five items and be results-oriented. The summary of qualifications is usually a list of short phrases. You can use a bulleted list, with each qualification on its own line. Or, to conserve space, you can arrange them in paragraph format, with a period after each one. Here's an example of a bulleted list:

Summary of Qualifications

- *Skilled copier sales manager/executive with nine years' sales experience and master's degree in business.*
- *Consistently surpassed annual revenue goals by 25 percent–plus.*
- *Named 2005 "Salesperson on the Year."*
- *Member of ABC Copiers' "Gold Key Circle" for exemplary sales achievements.*
- *Managed regional sales staff of 55.*

EXPERIENCE

The experience section is the heart of the chronological resume (we'll explain the functional resume format's related "Professional Experience" section on page 109). Its content can come from:

- ☼ Past jobs and accomplishments
- ☼ Freelancing/self-employment
- ☼ Initiatives you've launched/undertaken in or out of the office
- ☼ Training/education

☼ Awards won/goals met

☼ Activities

☼ Volunteer work

Remember that if you planned volunteer events or a neighborhood watch program, these activities involved skills that can be applied to the "work world" and should be counted as "experience" (because they require budgeting, negotiation, leadership, and so forth).

Here is part of a sample "Experience" section for a person seeking a corporate events director position.

Experience

Planned and executed unique, exciting events and trade shows for companies and individuals.

BIG CONSULTING CO., Boise, Idaho   2001–Present
Events Manager

Coordinated catering, audiovisual, event space, staffing, and supplies for 100+ meetings, parties, and trade shows each year.

- Skilled negotiator responsible for 16% savings on vendor contracts in 2005.
- Established and cultivated strong relationships with vendors and clients by seeing their every request was executed to the last detail.
- Increased number of quality trade-show leads by no less than 15% year after year.
- Secured top speakers for company events, including Sam Software, Barbara Broadcaster, and Gary Government. Oversaw related media requests and security.
- Treasurer, Boise Event Planners Association.

Note this job seeker's use of keywords, numbers, and well-known names. She uses an initial summary phrase explaining her experience. She sums up her relevant skills with bullet points (increasing revenue, exhibiting management skills, paying attention to detail). She also lists an office held in a professional organization—an achievement like this is perfectly acceptable to place higher up in the resume in the Experience section.

You may find that your most relevant achievements are from a past job. It's a common quandary—you have experience that relates to the position you are applying for, but it's not your most recent experience.

THINK Outside the Box

You Work Where?

Not everyone works for a recognized company. How do you explain on a resume what your company does if its name is vague or unknown (such as CGB, Inc., or TechLine Corp.)? Simply drop a brief description of the company into your description of your duties:

- **Marketing Director, ABC Corp.**
  Led marketing efforts for second-largest forklift distributor in the Southeast.

  This way you can clarify what your previous company did—and demonstrate what an industry leader it is, too!

If this is the case, you should still list your work experience chronologically, but if you have a particular experience that might give you a boost for a job, list it in a summary of qualifications at the top of your resume, as well as in the Experience section, *and* be sure to highlight that experience in your cover letter.

SKILLS

List your hard and soft skills here—especially the ones that relate to this job. Name specific software with which you are familiar; don't just say, "word processing," say, "Microsoft Word." Be sure to list any certifications you have earned, such as MCSE—these will definitely be keywords for technical positions, and resume-scanning software will be looking for them.

EDUCATION

Here is where you list your institution, your degree, and the year of your graduation. Some job seekers list their education ahead of experience on their resumes. This is perfectly fine if you sense that the employer values an applicant's educational background, you attended a top-tier school, or you received an award such as a Rhodes Scholarship. (In those cases, consider moving "Education" to the top of the resume, just beneath the "Objective Statement.")

Also be sure to list any "regular" educational awards you earned here, or higher on the resume if you feel they warrant such treatment—valedictorian, honorary degree, and so forth.

Do You List Your GPA?

Generally not. Once you are five to ten years into the working world, grades—good or bad—really don't matter anymore. However, if you graduated *magna cum laude* or with some other such distinction, you can include that with your degree information.

What If You Didn't Go to or Haven't Finished College?

Today people's educational tracks take more twists and turns than they used to, and HR professionals are well aware of this. List whatever schooling you have had from high school on up, as well as any separate training classes you've taken through past jobs or on your own. Then use the interview to show them how intelligent you really are!

What If You Changed Schools or Took More than Four Years to Graduate?

Again, don't sweat it. Just list the final school, degree, and the year you got it—the point is, you eventually *got* the degree.

Your Major

You may be asking yourself: Is my major really important? How crucial is it to my career in the grand scheme of things? The answer is . . . it depends.

In a Yahoo! HotJobs poll, two-thirds of job seekers said that they currently work in a field unrelated to their college major. The remaining third were employed in a field that was related to their major. Bottom line: Life and work experience outweigh a choice you made when you were nineteen.

FINISHING TOUCHES: AWARDS, MEMBERSHIPS, AND MORE

The final sections of your resume offer a bit more flexibility, depending on your experiences.

"Awards and Honors" is where you can list notable awards you have won, but that don't necessarily apply to your job—for example, State Judo Champion or Red

Cross Volunteer of the Month. They simply demonstrate other aspects of your skills. However, if the award correlates to the job, list it in the "Experience" section.

If you've done a lot of volunteer work, you might want to list it in a section titled **"Volunteer Work."** This applies to volunteer work you have done on a semi-regular basis. If that volunteer work involved more "working world" skills and more of your time—for example, you helped write press releases for a relief agency during a hurricane's aftermath, or you coordinated fund-raisers—you will want to list it higher up in the "Experience" section.

"Memberships/Certifications" is the section where you list your memberships in professional and civic associations as well as personal memberships (condo board, PTA). If you are an officer, you may want to list this higher on the resume.

You may choose to list your interests in an **"Activities"** section. These can help demonstrate your well-roundedness and self-motivation, as well as your depth of personality and additional skills. For example, you may enjoy teaching kids to swim (an activity you include on your resume), and it just so happens that the ad firm you are applying to is about to launch an ad campaign centered on getting kids to be more physically active. You never know.

However, avoid listing hobbies (knitting, reading, walking). They can rarely help your candidacy for a job and you may not be perceived as serious if you include them on your resume. If you're truly passionate about something, you can find a way to mention it in your interview.

Also, be cautious when mentioning affiliations with political or religious groups, activist organizations, and the like, unless they are specifically related to the job for which you are applying (teaching at a religious school, for example). (Similarly, if you have your own blog, you may want to avoid mentioning it either on your resume or during an interview.) Be yourself, of course—you don't want to work in an environment in which your beliefs aren't tolerated or respected. But unless your affiliations relate to the work, or perhaps you earned a leadership position within a religious or political group, you should refrain from mentioning these facts on your resume.

EXPERIENCE AND THE FUNCTIONAL FORMAT

Sections like Contact Information and Education look the same on both chrono-logical and functional resumes. However, your experience on a functional resume is presented differently. Functional resumes show your experiences grouped together, rather than broken out chronologically. This section can also be called "Relevant Experience" or "Professional Experience."

Here's an example of "experience" for a math teacher who has entered and left the workforce as he's encountered schooling and family events. While he doesn't mention the gaps here, he can always explain them in an interview.

PROFESSIONAL EXPERIENCE

Teaching
- Eight years' experience helping youths understand the mysteries and possibilities of math
- Certified in elementary- and secondary-level math
- Named "Math Teacher of the Year" for Drake Elementary (Robinson, Ohio) in 1994 and 1995
- Dedicated professional who believes nothing is more important than educating the next generation

Professional Development
- Participated in annual National Education Association "Math Matters!" Conference in 1995
- Sunday School teacher, second grade, Robinson United Methodist Church
- Certified in first aid/CPR

Leadership
- Launched and sponsored Robinson High School "Mathletes," who placed second in Ohio State Math Olympics
- Coached sixth-grade boys' and girls' basketball teams, Drake Elementary School

Child Development
- Developed and led after-school math tutoring program for students with C or lower average
- Full-time parent

FUNCTIONAL FORMAT AND WORK HISTORY

Although you do need to list your work history on a functional resume, this time it's very basic—employers, locations, and years of service. You can omit jobs that were short term or don't demonstrate upward movement. And feel free to list parenting and volunteer work.

Continuing with our teacher example:

2003–2006	Full-time Parent
1996–2003	Robinson High School, Robinson, Ohio—Trigonometry teacher, grades 9–12
1994–1995	Drake Elementary, Robinson, Ohio—Sixth-grade teacher
1992–1994	The Ohio State University—Full-time master's student
1991–1992	Chester Junior High, Robinson, Ohio—Sixth-grade teacher

Should You Use a Professional Resume Writer?

If you find a reputable one, and have the means, then it's certainly worth a try. Also, if you know your writing isn't very strong, or English is not your first language, you may want to consider getting professional help. Otherwise, there are many books and Internet articles and templates that can guide you.

If you would feel better with a pro, select a reputable company with a proven track record, such as ResumeEdge (http://hotjobs.resumeedge.com). Or look for someone who is a member of a professional resume writers association, such as the Professional Association of Resume Writers & Career Coaches (PARW/CC).

take a memo

Watch Your Words

Four phrases every resume should include:

- ☼ **Teamwork** or **team player:** It's more important in the workplace now than ever.
- ☼ **Detail-oriented:** This phrase shows you won't let things fall through the cracks.
- ☼ **Self-motivated** or **self-starter:** You can generate your own ideas and follow them through to fruition.
- ☼ **Flexible:** Malleable employees who can "roll" with changes quickly are valuable.

Words to avoid:

- ☼ **Abbreviations and acronyms** (unless they are recognized terms such as BA, C++, or MCSE): Write out school names (State University, not "SU") and full names of volunteer organizations.
- ☼ **Personal pronouns:** Your resume is all about you; the addition of "I" or "me" is redundant.
- ☼ **Negative words:** Words such as "arrested," "boring," "failed," and "fired" will catch recruiters' attention for the wrong reason. These terms refer to issues you can raise during the interview if necessary.
- ☼ **Articles and abused words:** *a, also, an, because, the, very, successfully*—of course you performed a task successfully, or it wouldn't be on your resume in the first place!

OTHER STICKY QUESTIONS

Some questions relating to format and ethics are tough—here's some help.

Months versus Years in a Position

This question has come up more in recent years after the advent of the Internet economy had many workers "job-hopping." Listing years (2001–2003) alone is fine; however, the more specific you can be about time spent at each job, the better. If you only spent a few months at a job, it's fine to list it if the job is relevant (April–September 2002); otherwise, you can leave it off. A recruiter is not going to balk at three months missing from your resume. However . . .

What If I've Got Large Gaps in My Work History?

As we've mentioned, people's career paths are twisting more than ever before. And with the increase of adoption aid, family and medical leave, and home-schooling, as well as corporate downsizing, having gaps on a resume isn't necessarily a red flag. Use the functional resume format to emphasize your skills and experience, also pulling from the skills you learned during the gaps (for example, you may have learned how to do "scheduling" as a result of caring for twins). If you have noticeable gaps on your resume, be prepared to explain them in an interview, if asked.

What If I Was Fired?

Everyone makes mistakes, but being fired doesn't look so good in black and white. Consider listing the experience without listing the outcome. Or, leave it off altogether. Be prepared to explain in an interview why you left the job, if asked.

Is It OK to "Fudge" Things on a Resume?

No, no, and no. Today, when employers perform all sorts of background and reference checks, fudging on a resume can catch up with you—even if it's several years down the road. The truth always has a way of getting out. However, keep in mind that certain omissions *are* acceptable on a resume today, such as jobs you held more than ten years before (or a job you only held for three months before being fired or laid off) if they aren't relevant to the job you're applying for.

Take a lesson from these famous downfalls:

☼ In 2004, James Minder, CEO of Smith & Wesson Holding Corp., resigned after it was revealed that he had served fifteen years in prison for several armed robberies.

- ☼ In 2002, Quincy Troupe, California's first poet laureate, stepped down after a background check showed that he hadn't graduated from college as he'd claimed.
- ☼ In 2001, Coach George O'Leary resigned from Notre Dame's football program just days after joining. Having claimed he'd earned a master's degree in education and played college football for three years, O'Leary admitted it wasn't true.

Do I Include References?

Not on the resume. If a job ad asks for references, supply them on a separate sheet. Don't wait until you're asked to get your references together, however. You should be sure all the people you will be using as references know they might be called, and that each one will indeed say good things about you. Remember that crotchety former manager? He might not be the best reference for you—or anyone else.

What if the Job Posting Asks for My Salary Requirements?

There's a general rule not to mention salary before an interview because your desired salary may be too high and put you out of the running; alternately, specifying a lower salary than the company is prepared to offer will shortchange you. However, if specifically asked, you need to put something down. As we mentioned in chapter 6, if necessary, always put salary requirements in the cover letter, never in the resume. If you're feeling flexible, you could put "negotiable." This should at least prevent you from being excluded from the first round of consideration. If you do have a salary requirement as a result of financial commitments, then consider listing a salary range.

Remember, your resume should be a living, breathing document. Revisit it frequently, and add to your resume as you acquire new skills and experiences.

Lily Jones

123 Spruce Lane
Boise, Idaho 83702
555-555-5555

lily_m_jones@yahoo.com

Summary Statement

Talented event planner with a flair for creating memorable corporate and private events. Resourceful and skilled negotiator known for bringing meetings, trade shows, and parties in on schedule and at or under budget.

Experience

Planned and executed unique, exciting events and trade shows for companies and individuals.

BIG CONSULTING CO., Boise, Idaho   2001–Present
Events Manager

Coordinated catering, audiovisual, event space, staffing, and supplies for 100+ meetings, parties, and trade shows each year.

- Skilled negotiator responsible for 16% savings on vendor contracts in 2005.
- Established and cultivated strong relationships with vendors and clients by seeing their every request was executed to the last detail.
- Increased number of quality trade-show leads by no less than 15% year after year.
- Secured top speakers for company events, including Sam Software, Barbara Broadcaster, and Gary Government. Oversaw related media requests and security.
- Managed staff of three.

WONDERFUL WEDDINGS AND EVENTS (WWE), New Orleans, Louisiana   1995–2001
Catering Manager

Ensured that meals for the biggest days in the lives of our clients were beautiful, affordable— and delicious!

- Oversaw hiring, ordering, preparation, and serving of meals for more than 300 weddings and ceremonies.
- Implemented Web-based ordering system for bulk food supplies, saving WWE more than 20% per year.
- First caterer in New Orleans to offer kosher and all-vegetarian menus for clients.
- Catered for more than 600 guests at wedding of daughter of New Orleans Mayor.
- Managed all WWE alcohol and health certification and training.

Lily Jones   Page two

NEW ORLEANS TOURISM GROUP, New Orleans, Louisiana   1992–1995
Associate

Worked to promote the history, hospitality, and culture of the Crescent City and entice businesses and families to visit.

- Co-developed the award-winning "More Than Mardi Gras" print advertising campaign, which garnered over $5 million in tourist dollars in 1994.
- Assisted media in placing positive stories about New Orleans in business and mainstream publications.
- Managed daily updates to Web site.

THOMAS TAVERN RESTAURANT, Boise Idaho   Summers 1988–1992
Server

Provided premier customer service in four-star restaurant.

- Won "Employee of the Month" award three times.
- Trained six new employees, two of whom were promoted.

Skills

Food and floral preparation, negotiation, project management, FoodPro Plus, fluent in Spanish and French, Microsoft 95/98/2000/XP/Office, Excel, PowerPoint.

Education

- MBA, Louisiana State University, Baton Rouge, 1992
- BA, Culinary Arts, Johnson and Wales, Charleston, SC, 1990

Memberships

- Treasurer, Boise Event Planners Association
- American Event Planners Association
- Boise Event Planners Association
- American Florists Association
- Association of Bridal Consultants

Volunteer Work

Red Cross, New Orleans Chapter   2005

Arranged food preparation and delivery after Hurricane Katrina

Thomas Kay

235 Barton Street ◆ Miami, Florida 33139
555-555-5555 ◆ thomas_kay2000@yahoo.com

OBJECTIVE STATEMENT

Seeking a fund-raising position with a nonprofit, where I can dedicate my background in finance and biology to the protection of endangered species.

PROFESSIONAL EXPERIENCE

Fund-raising
- Responsible for more than $400,000 in individual donations in 2005. (The Everglades Fund)
- Led four tours of 15+ donors each through the Everglades to give a hands-on understanding of where their money was going. (The Everglades Fund)
- As a campaign fund-raiser, produced promotional events that raised funds and generated public support. (Erwin Fletcher Mayoral Campaign, Miami, Florida)

Grant Writing
- Secured more than $250,000 from top companies including International Automobiles and Superior Shipping toward the refurbishment of the Miami Zoo reptile house. (Miami Zoological Park)
- Turned several one-time donors into repeat donors, resulting in $25,000 extra for the zoo over two years. (Miami Zoological Park)

Communication
- Excellent research and writing capabilities. Articulate ideas clearly and concisely.
- Used listening and verbal skills to relate the plight of the Everglades to potential donors from diverse backgrounds.
- Through proposals, reports, and correspondence, persuaded individuals and decision makers within the government and private sectors to recognize and respond to the threats to the Everglades from developers and poachers.
- Handled media relations, providing an accurate and concise portrayal of candidate's positions on current issues. (Erwin Fletcher Mayoral Campaign, Miami, Florida)
- Contribute articles to *Florida Nature Lover's Magazine*.

WORK HISTORY

2002-2005	The Everglades Fund, Naples, Florida
2002	Campaign Fund-raising Manager, Erwin Fletcher Mayoral Campaign, Miami, Florida
1995–2001	Miami Zoological Park, Miami, Florida

PROFESSIONAL DEVELOPMENT AND EDUCATION

Treasurer, Florida Audubon Society, 2004–Present
Boy Scout Troop Leader, 2000–2005
MS, Biology, University of Miami, 1994
BA, cum laude, Finance, University of Miami, Miami, FL, 1992

Recommended Books

Resumes for Dummies by Joyce Lain Kennedy (John Wiley & Sons, 2002, ISBN 0764554719, $16.99).

Resumes That Knock 'em Dead (Knock 'em Dead Series) by Martin Yate (Adams Media Corporation, 2004, ISBN 159337108X, $12.95).

Damn Good Resume Guide: A Crash Course in Resume Writing by Yana Parker (Ten Speed Press, 2002, ISBN 1580084443, $9.95).

The Resume Handbook: How to Write Outstanding Resumes & Cover Letters for Every Situation by Arthur D. Rosenberg & David Hizer (Adams Media Corporation, 2003, ISBN 1580628540, $9.95).

Recommended Web Sites

Yahoo! HotJobs—Resume Writing:
http://hotjobs.yahoo.com/resume

Rockport Institute's How to Write a Masterpiece of a Resume:
www.rockportinstitute.com/resumes.html

ResumeEdge:
http://hotjobs.resumeedge.com

ResumeTutor:
www.umn.edu/ohr/ecep/resume

Loyola University Chicago's Guide for Writing Effective Resumes:
www.luc.edu/resources/career/resguide.pdf

CHAPTER 8

Face to Face: Interviewing and the Hiring Process

"And, finally, are you now or have you ever been disgruntled?"

Poison ivy? Running into your ex? Arriving late for your best friend's wedding? Compared to the average job interview, these situations may sound like welcome events. For some reason, no matter how experienced you are, job interviews never seem to get any easier.

Sure, you've had a few interviews by now, so you know the basics. And unlike when you were just out of college, you now bring more value to the table. You've also learned that the interviewer is not some great and powerful being, but merely another professional, just like you, looking to make a good fit.

However, now that you are further along in your career, interviews are going to be tougher and more thorough than those you've had before. You'll need to be able to convey your work experience and accomplishments, as they relate to the new company, in a clear manner, with facts and figures to back them up.

Also, as with resumes, there are those nagging questions that are classic quandaries for job seekers at any level: *Is it acceptable to call the recruiter to follow up after the interview? What if I have gaps in my work history?*

You can take control of the interview before it even starts by being prepared. In this chapter we'll discuss how to make a great impression on interviewers by clearly explaining how your experience fits the company's needs, gracefully tackling difficult interview questions, and voicing your own personality and inquiries. We'll review the different types of interviews, and essential etiquette for each. But before we get started, let's take a quick refresher course on how the hiring process works.

WHO YA GONNA CALL? UNDERSTANDING THE HIRING PROCESS

Job seekers may think they understand the hiring process, but statistics show that recruiters and job hunters are not always on the same page. The confusion is understandable. The hiring process is more convoluted than it appears—many factors and people, not to mention time and money, are at work in filling a position. Let's take a look at the various people you'll be meeting throughout the process.

Jack (or Jill) of All Trades: The Recruiter

The recruiter is a hiring specialist who works with a hiring manager to bring two people—you and the hiring manager—together. Her duties are many: gathering the required skills from the hiring manager, screening resumes, scheduling interviews, helping candidates navigate the hiring process, and making the offer. In smaller companies she may wear even more hats. She usually is working to fill several jobs at once, so her time is limited. But she is a great resource on company culture and benefits.

He Said/She Said

A Yahoo! HotJobs poll asked job seekers, "Do you feel you understand how the hiring process works?" The majority—62 percent—replied "Yes." But when we asked recruiters a similar question—"Do you feel that job seekers understand the hiring process?"—a whopping 75 percent responded "No."

Your Boss-to-Be: The Hiring Manager

Hiring manager is a role a supervisor performs when a position opens up in his department. While working to fill the position, he still maintains his regular job. Therefore, hiring managers have a limited amount of time to spend on hiring. So sometimes, due to time pressures or other commitments, a hiring manager will farm out the job of interviewing to a direct report. In this case, you should consider it your main priority to impress this interviewer.

The Major Manager (The Boss' Boss)

The hiring manager's boss wants to make sure his direct report is considering qualified candidates. Because of your level of experience, it's likely you will be working closely with this person at some point, so chances are you will meet her during your interview rounds. Depending on her time and respect for subordinates, she may ask you easy questions ("So, why would you like to work here?") or toughies ("What do you think caused the 10 percent drop in our stock price last month?"). So be prepared.

Potential Peers

You will also likely meet with some of your potential coworkers. They may ultimately be above or beneath you in level, but treat all of them as professionally as you do the hiring manager. They may not have good interviewing skills, but their opinions of your personality and enthusiasm will count. Put your best foot forward.

take a memo

Avoid Q&A Faux Pas at the Job Interview

Job candidates who confuse the roles of recruiter and hiring manager often ask the wrong question of the wrong person and wind up ruining otherwise great interviews.

Here are some important clarifications:

The **recruiter** is your general resource for company information. Pitch the recruiter questions about company culture and employee benefits, including health insurance and 401(k) plans. You can ask about standard vacation time, but keep upcoming vacation plans to yourself—it can leave a bad impression.

Because the recruiter oversees the administrative duties associated with filling open positions, you can certainly ask her about the next steps in the process. The recruiter will also be able to tell you who your primary contact will be. Make sure you get this person's name, title, phone number, and e-mail address.

The **hiring manager** is the ideal person to answer any questions you have about the specifics of the position, including the day-to-day responsibilities. You should also ask intelligent questions that show that you have researched the company and, if possible, the department the hiring manager oversees.

Be prepared to demonstrate an understanding of what the company does—if the firm has a Web site, spend some time there reading bios of senior management and recent press releases. Avoid asking the hiring manager questions about benefits—these should be reserved for the recruiter.

Your Gateway: The Receptionist

There's one more important person to keep in mind: the receptionist. Remember that the interview begins as soon as you walk through the door. The receptionist will likely be the first person you encounter as you wait for the human resources representative or hiring manager to come for you. Be polite, of course, and treat him as professionally as you would the other people you meet.

MUSICAL CHAIRS—FOR EVERYONE

At times the hiring process can seem like a game of musical chairs at a childhood birthday party—you dress up and run around and around trying to beat out the other contestants, while the hiring manager controls the music.

If it's any consolation, the hiring manager has quite a bit to worry about, too. Hiring is very costly to a company, and bad hires can cost even more. And with the evolution of performance reviews, feedback, and the "360-degree review" (in which peers review both peers and managers), managers are highly account-able for who they bring in and the new hire's performance.

This is why the hiring process has so many levels. It actually begins before you even enter the picture. First, the hiring manager lets the recruiter know he needs to fill a position. They work together to come up with the proper skills, level, title, and possibly salary/benefits to list in the job posting. The recruiter will then post the job online and/or in the newspaper.

Next, you spot the listing and submit your resume and cover letter for the job. The first person to receive that information is the recruiter. She will screen all the incoming resumes (sometimes hundreds depending on the job and the size of the company) for the ones that best fit the desired skills and experience—as well as those with the best organization and grammar.

If you make the cut, you'll receive a call from the recruiter. If she does a phone screen, she'll ask you basic questions about your skills and interest in the position. If there is a potential match, she will arrange an in-person interview for you with the hiring manager. Or, she may just skip the phone screen and set up an interview right away.

When you come in for the interview, you'll first meet with the recruiter, who will then take you to meet the hiring manager. He will likely ask you probing questions about what you can do for the department and the company, and what your long-term goals are. From there you might be finished, or you might meet the hiring manager's boss and your prospective coworkers. If these interviews go well, there might be a second or third interview, if necessary.

Over the next few days or weeks, the recruiter will be checking your refer-ences—calling the list of former supervisors and colleagues you have provided to confirm that you would be a worthy employee. If those reference checks go well, further checks might be performed, such as a credit check, a background check, and even a drug test. The recruiter will also meet with the hiring manager for his thoughts about the candidates for the position. Finally, the recruiter will call and (hopefully) make you an offer.

TYPES OF INTERVIEWS

Now let's talk about interviews specifically. Just as there are several people involved in the hiring process, there are also several types of interviews—and in your job search, you might encounter all of them.

Traditional

You've probably experienced this type of interview several times before. You talk with the hiring manager for a half-hour to an hour, and possibly with other members of the department. You discuss your work history and experience,

take a memo

Phone Interview Tips

Although on the phone you might feel safer with some distance between yourself and your interviewer, you still should be just as professional as if the person were in the same room with you.

- ☼ Find a quiet place to take the call, away from the computer, the TV, loud roommates, screaming children, family dogs, or other distractions.

- ☼ If it's not a good time for you to talk, say so—the recruiter will understand. Let the recruiter know how pleased you are that he called, confirm his callback number, and then reschedule for a time in the near future when you will be able to focus your undivided attention on his call.

- ☼ Have your resume and a pen and paper handy.

- ☼ Be positive and enthusiastic—try to smile while you're talking. Interviewers can hear it in your voice, and it will boost your mood and calm your nerves.

- ☼ Stand up—this will make you feel more confident.

- ☼ Listen carefully to your interviewer's questions, and his responses to your answers. Take notes.

- ☼ Have some questions prepared for the inevitable, "Do you have any questions?"

- ☼ Practice a phone interview with a friend ahead of time.

your education, and the reasons why you're interested in the company. You find out about the company culture, the team you could potentially be working with, and perhaps potential compensation packages.

Phone Interviews

Sometimes the recruiter's call itself may be an initial interview, so treat it as if it were a formal interview. You might even get a call from the hiring manager. Take the call someplace quiet and private—if you need to call back later, make arrangements to speak at another time. (See "Phone Interview Tips" on page 124 for useful strategies for this type of interview.)

Group Interviews

Group interviews—in which you'll meet with two or more people at once—can be nerve-racking. But don't see it as being "ganged-up" on; rather, consider it an opportunity to impress several people at once! *Interesting fact:* In some countries, it's common for the interviewer to meet with multiple *candidates* at once. At least this way you're the only one in the room vying for a job!

Treat each interviewer as if she would be your manager. Make eye contact with the individual asking the question and then each person in the group as you answer. Smile and try to connect topics to the people asking about them— feel free to take brief notes to help you organize your thoughts. Focus on one question at a time, and don't worry about what's coming next. Listen, and don't interrupt.

Meal Interviews

At this point in your career, it's quite possible you'll be invited to a meal interview with the hiring manager. While you may be getting free grub, meal interviews offer their own set of considerations on top of the usual interview worries. Not only do you have to give good answers—but now you have to give them between bites! Here are some handy tips for mastering the meal interview:

- ☼ Brush up on basic table manners—scan the definitive book on the subject, *Emily Post's Etiquette.*
- ☼ Avoid messy foods like burgers or spaghetti, and do not order alcohol, even if your interviewer does—you want to be clear-headed.
- ☼ Order a medium-priced menu item and no dessert (coffee, however, is fine).

- ☼ Have a snack beforehand—that way, you won't be hungry going into the meal. You'll feel better as the interview begins, and more alert as you're talking about your background.
- ☼ Don't offer to pay for the meal—it's not expected.
- ☼ The best rule of thumb is to follow the interviewer's lead.

Case-Based Interviews

In certain professions, like finance and consulting, you may be given a real-life or simulated business problem and asked to form a plan for solving it. These interviews require in-depth analysis and industry knowledge. To prepare, you can read sample case studies of companies online, as well as trade magazines, newspapers, and Yahoo! Finance to be on top of the latest news and trends.

take a memo

Case in Point

In responding to case-based interview questions, you should do more than parrot broad theories—you need to craft a well-thought-out plan and analysis, as well as offer recommendations for solutions. To do this:

- ☼ Read the problem and break it into smaller pieces.
- ☼ Decide which areas are higher priority and address those first.
- ☼ Give clear analytic evidence, using assumptions, previous experience, math (if applicable), and logic.
- ☼ Make a real recommendation designed to generate results.

PREPARING FOR AN INTERVIEW

When you went on your first interview, you probably worried most about whether or not you had broccoli in your teeth.

But now, as an experienced worker, you have a lot more territory to cover, more responsibilities to account for, and maybe even some rough spots in your career history to explain. You need to have hard numbers to back up your successes. The expectations are higher for you to demonstrate why you deserve a position. As an experienced worker, you're going to be expected to show why you are the best choice.

In his excellent book *101 Great Answers to the Toughest Interview Questions*, author Ron Fry suggests focusing on:

☼ Your key accomplishments at previous jobs.

☼ The strengths demonstrated by those accomplishments.

☼ How these relate to the job for which you're applying.

In order to handle all these issues in an interview, you need to be prepared—both mentally and on paper—and able to manage tough questions about your past and your future.

take a **memo**

Additional Interview Tasks

In addition to the interview itself, you may be asked to take a variety of tests. These can be scheduled for the day of the interview, on a different day, or even taken at home. Work with the recruiter to set a schedule that helps you perform your best at all elements of the interview.

Aptitude Tests: These are tests that assess your grasp of specific skills, such as programming, writing, or editing.

Integrity Tests: These tests examine a candidate's judgment and atti-tude—for example, propensity for anger, honesty, and ability to take direction. Candidates for jobs involving finances or sensitive information might be required to take these kinds of tests.

Personality/Psychological Tests: As we discussed in chapter 1, person-ality tests are a way to gauge a person's likes, dislikes, and work style. While they aren't a concrete measure of work ability, these tests are sometimes used in professions where personality and people skills are key, such as sales. Psychological tests can be used for high-pressure fields like law enforcement.

There is some controversy over whether these types of tests are accurate, fair, or even useful. However, the Equal Employment Opportunity Commission does generally deem this sort of testing as legal, so you may encounter it. If you're unsure about a test or its results, ask how the results will be used, get feedback after the test is scored, and request assurance that your results will be kept confidential.

▶**Action Items:** Hire Education

Have you ever interviewed anyone before? If so, think back to that experience. What impressed you about the person you eventually hired? What qualities were you looking for? What red flags did you pick up? If you've never interviewed anyone, imagine that you are hiring someone to work for you—to clean your house, to baby-sit your kids, or to assist you at your current job. What qualities would be important to you? Are these qualities you feel that you yourself possess?

Your Personal Portfolio

As we discussed in chapter 7, you can't pack all your experiences and achievements into your resume. In order to remember and explain all the great accomplishments that make you a good hire for this job, you need to have tangible records of them. A personal portfolio helps you keep track of the qualities that make you stand out (and gives you a bit of a cheat sheet during the actual interview).

In addition to your resume, create a bullet-pointed list of the facts you really want to get across—including business accomplishments such as "youngest manager ever hired in the mergers and acquisitions division" or "landed six new clients in fourth quarter." If it comes up in your conversation, you may also want to mention personal achievements, such as "completed my first triathlon two minutes under my goal." You can use these personal accomplishments as examples to support the successes on your resume.

Also, be sure to have any work samples with you, if applicable—and enough copies both for you and all your interviewers. Look over these samples ahead of time and make notes as to why they make you stand out. Did the graphic you designed for your last company help increase sales 14 percent? Did the press release you wrote for a new product get story placement in a major newspaper? These are the important accomplishments that are easy to forget during an interview.

Mental Preparation

You also need to be *mentally* prepared for an interview. Have the facts and figures that tie you and your experience to this potential job at the forefront of your mind, so that you can recall them easily if the right question comes along.

First, you need to practice your "elevator speech" (see page 47)—and remember it as you go into the interview. It will help you remember your strong points and build your confidence. For example:

I am a great teacher. My students love me because I take an interest in their lives outside the classroom. But I believe that students need to take responsibility for their own education—no one can do it for them. I support them in everything they do.

Also, memorize your own "stats," just as you might those for a sports team: "I brought in four new clients last year, increasing sales by 10 percent or $50,000"; "I launched a direct mail campaign that saw an 11 percent response rate"; "I saved $3 million in one year by making cost reductions achieved through contract negotiations."

Be aware of trends in your industry. Read newspapers and trade journals for the latest news and tips, and keep those in mind as you do your interviews. Also, use your research on the position, the hiring manager, and the company to present yourself as the type of candidate who would fit in there.

take a memo

Ask the Expert: What Employers *Really* Want

Job hunters often have difficulty understanding what an employer is looking for, and how to present themselves successfully. According to David L. Dunkel, Chairman and CEO of Kforce Professional Staffing, the most successful job applicants will demonstrate these traits:

- A blend of innate and acquired skills. Intelligent people can always learn the hard/technical skills, but someone with no interpersonal skills will create problems in an organization. And, the higher you progress within an organization, the more important and valued your soft skills will be.

- Specific subject matter expertise and the ability to apply it to solve business problems

- Ability to work in a team setting to achieve results

- Demonstration of the value brought to former employers through a successful track record

- Positive, enthusiastic references

Anticipate Trouble

Even the best employees have had some detours along their career paths, including layoffs, pregnancies, or leaving work to go to school full time. Such gaps may raise questions. So be ready. If you have a noticeable period of time in which you didn't work, have a direct, honest, and professional answer prepared:

- ☀ "I left my previous job because of a family member's illness."
- ☀ "My wife and I decided to start a family, so I took two years off to raise our son."
- ☀ "I was laid off because my previous company merged with a larger firm and my department was eliminated. In the meantime I have been volunteering with Special Olympics and active with the local Chamber of Commerce."
- ☀ "I decided that pursuing my master's degree made more sense at the time."

Don't be embarrassed to discuss your career's odd twists and turns—the hiring manager most likely has gaps in her own resume. Nor should you chide yourself for past mistakes; instead, explain what you learned about yourself and your industry as a result of these experiences. If you realize now that a decision to leave or change jobs was wrong, it's okay to say so—this demonstrates humility, insight, maturity, and the ability to grow as a person. The collective choices you've made have brought you to where you are today.

By the same token, you might have had a number of jobs in a short period—not uncommon after the Internet bubble burst. Job-hopping is far more acceptable now than in our parents' era. Still, you should be prepared:

- ☀ "I sought challenges with a new and different start-up company; however, the firm ultimately lacked the funding to continue. But I learned a great deal in my short time there."

Or,

- ☀ "At that time industry trends indicated that Web-based widgets were the next big thing. Unfortunately, we were wrong, but working for Widgets, Inc., was still a great experience for me and taught me a lot about the widget industry—knowledge I can now apply to your company."

INTERVIEW GOALS

An interview is not a one-way street. It should not be the employer grilling you, but a chance for you both to get to know each other and see if you'd make a good fit.

Basically, a hiring manager is trying to answer three fundamental questions:

1. Are you qualified for the job?
2. Will you fit into his company's culture?
3. How can you help solve specific problems facing the department?

You, too, have some goals:

1. To convey your skills and abilities as they relate to the new company.
2. To get a sense of what it would be like working with these people—do your personalities mesh?
3. To ask questions of your own, both to solicit information and to demonstrate that you have done your homework.
4. To find out what they are offering in compensation without tipping your hand about the salary you'd like to receive.

At the end of an interview, an employer should know whether she wants your candidacy to proceed, and you should know whether you still *want* to proceed. Sometimes you'll find that a job is everything you wanted and more—and therefore you may need to do more practicing and research to be ready for a second interview or an offer, if it comes. Or you may realize that a job is not suited for you—and that's okay, too. That is what an interview is for.

JOB QUALIFICATIONS

Now it's time to focus on the most important part of the interview—the discussion of your qualifications. Whether you're meeting with the recruiter or the hiring manager, first and foremost, the interviewer is interested in whether or not you are *qualified for the job*. Clearly, they *think* you are or you wouldn't be here—but now is your chance to dispel any doubt from their minds.

As we've said, the best way to do this is by using hard facts and numbers to prove your worth—clients you've acquired, number of products you've sold, records you've broken, turnover you've lowered, and so on. Much of this is already on your resume, but now you want to reiterate your biggest accomplishments—and add further detail. Fortunately, you've already prepared to do this.

For example, one of the first questions the interviewer asks might be, "Why do you want to work at XYZ, Inc.?"

Even with a broad, icebreaking question like this, you want to say something besides, "It seems like a fun place to work." Instead, you might reply:

> *I feel with the experience I gained as a sales leader for Acme, Inc., it was time to expand into a more challenging area—and why not do it with a company that has led its sector for the last five years?*

Here you've already begun elaborating on your skills *and* shown that you've been following this new company.

Next, he'll begin asking questions that get at the heart of your resume, asking for more detail on those most interesting and relevant parts, as well as any perceived gaps in your experience or required skills that you may be lacking. For example:

- ☼ "You say that as a project manager, you made sure that projects you oversaw were completed an average of two days ahead of schedule. How did you accomplish this?"
- ☼ "You're skilled in Software Design 4.2. Have you had much experience with Design Pro 3.1?"
- ☼ "Explain your technique for closing a sale."

Listen carefully to the questions and don't be afraid to ask for clarification, if necessary. Use keywords from the job ad as you answer.

For example, let's say Ann is applying to work in the public relations department of a large company. The job ad asks for an "efficient, organized" person to increase story placements. She is asked, "What makes you qualified for this position?" and responds:

> *Because I know how to present fresh angles that get attention for my clients.* **[This sums up in one sentence what makes her a valuable PR professional—getting** *publicity.]* You'll see on my resume that as assistant *public relations manager for the retail store Sports Stuff, last quarter I had two stories placed with major market newspapers in one week. I am efficient and organized, which makes my company's, and the reporters', jobs easier.* **[Relates numbers and keywords to exactly how she would help the new company.]**

Other questions for this portion of the interview could be:

- ☼ "How have you used PhotoEditor 2.4 in your past positions?"
- ☼ "I see you began your IT career as a programmer. What makes you want to be an IT director?"

☼ "We're working on developing a new type of board game. How might the user testing you've performed at your previous job help us determine whether the game will be successful with kids ages 8–12?"

Finally, be prepared for an amateur interviewer. Due to nervousness or inexperience, an interviewer may neglect to ask you anything of substance. If the hiring manager doesn't ask the right interview questions, it's up to you to communicate your qualifications during the interview. So have them in mind and bring them up yourself, even if the interviewer isn't asking you about them.

FILLING IN THE BLANKS

Your interviewer will also ask you about things you haven't accomplished (yet), and may possibly inquire further into potential red flags. Being positive and willing to learn will help you smooth over these rough edges.

Career Gaps

As we mentioned earlier, if the career gap or job-hopping issues come up, the best way to handle them is with preparation and honesty. You can also put a positive spin on a bad situation by emphasizing what you learned from it. For example:

> As much as I disliked being laid off from College Textbooks, Inc., that gave me the chance to finish my degree—which has equipped me to take on new challenges and help my next company succeed.

Why Are You Here?

Another common question is, "Why do you want to leave your current job?" It could be for a number of reasons, as we discussed in chapter 1. Maybe you've outgrown it, maybe you dislike your manager, or maybe you flat-out just hate the job.

The point is, you don't want to be negative, and you especially don't want to badmouth your current (or any former) company or manager. Even if it's deserved, it makes you look petty—and you never know if the hiring manager might know your former boss. So instead, frame your departure in a positive light:

☼ "I feel I have outgrown my position and am ready for new challenges."

☼ "The chances of advancement in that company are limited, and I'm looking to move ahead."

☀ "I want to find a position in which I can both learn and lead at the same time."

Missing Skills

You can only be the best candidate you can be—no one is perfectly and immediately going to fit the mold of what the new company is looking for. You will still have some catching up to do. For missing skills, again, a positive spin can help:

I don't have training in Content Management Pro 4.2, but I am a fast learner. And I am familiar with Content King 3.0, skills I'm sure I could adapt to the program you use here.

Remember, they wouldn't have called you for the interview if they didn't feel your other skills and experience made you a good fit for the position.

PERSONALITY AND COMPANY CULTURE

As an interviewer probes into your "hard" skills and qualifications for the job, he'll also want to find out more about your personality and passion for the job, asking such questions as:

☀ "What kind of approach do you take when it comes to managing others?"

☀ "Our department has recently undergone some significant reorganization. What is your approach for adapting to change?"

☀ "Do you prefer to work independently or have more regular contact with teammates?"

Your answers can reveal much about your attitude and work ethic. There is no wrong answer as long as you are upbeat and convey that you are capable of learning from difficult situations.

In fact, this portion of the interview allows you more freedom in your answers. Rather than focusing on your quantifiable accomplishments, you can simply be yourself. For example:

☀ "I find that I work well within the structure and camaraderie of an office environment. I enjoy interacting with others."

☀ "I enjoy volunteering not only because it has taught me skills I can use in the business world, but also because it helps me keep things in perspective, and I like helping people."

And if you have something you want to say but the opportunity has not come up yet, by all means, segue (carefully) into this topic during the conversation:

- ☼ "I'd like to pick up on your earlier question about teamwork. Along with three other coworkers, I launched an adopt-a-classroom initiative in which we tutored twenty kids each week at a local elementary school."

The interviewer will also want to see how you'd fit into the company culture. Questions that delve into that include:

- ☼ "How do you handle disagreement or conflict?"
- ☼ "How do you feel about working weekends?"
- ☼ "We just expanded our department by about twenty people, so communication is really key right now. How do you make sure your manager and teammates are up to speed on what you are working on?"

Remember not to get defensive, and be honest with yourself about what you need from company culture. Don't say that you can work eighty hours a week if you have two toddlers at home and want to spend quality time with your family.

Finally, as you and your interviewer get to know each other, be sure not to get so off track discussing your mutual interest in a sports team or a common hobby that you run out of time to talk about you! This can often happen with inexperienced interviewers. Always try to steer the conversation back to *how you are qualified for the job.*

THE OLD STANDBYS

By now we've covered some of the tough situations and questions you might encounter in an interview: how to deal with career gaps, how to explain being fired, why you left your previous job, and so on.

In addition, you'll probably be asked some of the more traditional questions ("Tell me about yourself")—which will require incorporating your job and life experience into your answers. Here are some stumpers that often come up at interviews—and some sample answers:

"Tell Me a Little about Yourself."

Sometimes the most general question can be the hardest. How can you sum up your entire life story in just a couple of minutes? You don't. With a question like this, you need to look at the subtext—the question behind the question. The interviewer is not asking about your hobbies or your family. Instead, he's asking you to describe what you can offer the company.

The point is not to summarize your resume—the interviewer already has a copy of that. Rather, explain how you came to be interested in this particular company and job, and weave examples of past accomplishments throughout to demonstrate why you are the perfect candidate for this job.

You might say:

I am a salesperson who is best motivated by a challenge. That's why I have decided to look into your company and the XYZ industry. I had a great record at my previous company, becoming the second-best salesperson of all time in my division. I develop strong relationships with clients and I bend over backwards to help them get what they need. Now I want to draw on my skills to sell XYZ, and to lead others to do the same.

"What Is Your Biggest Weakness?"

One of the great things about being in the workforce is discovering strengths you never knew you had. And by now you're probably familiar with some areas that could use improvement, too! Your potential employer may want to know what those areas are to get a better understanding of how you deal with challenges.

If faced with this question, you should be honest. No, we don't mean "I tend to get crazy at company parties" or "I steal office supplies." Nor should you be insincere: "I work too many weekends." Instead, discuss a quality that makes you look like a champ for recognizing and attempting to correct it.

For example:

- ☼ "I haven't always been successful at having a healthy work-life balance. I'm learning how to better balance things so that I am not only a more productive worker, but healthier too."

- ☼ "Sometimes I want so much to demonstrate to a client that I am listening that I don't write down what was said. Now I use a digital recorder to take notes so that I can focus on the client but still have a detailed record of his needs afterwards."

- ☼ "I naturally prefer to work alone and take care of tasks myself, but this can be really stressful. I'm finding that delegating work gets things done thoroughly and more quickly."

Remember to pick a "weakness" that, despite being a flaw, will still speak strongly of your skills.

"Where Do You See Yourself in Five Years?"

No, you don't have to say, "Right here at XYZ, Inc." Instead, the best tactic is to discuss your values and how your job will accommodate them.

Don't get too detailed about your specific career plan—or how that plan would take you away from this company. *Don't* give details about your plans for a family, or how you'd like to go back to school full time. Instead, discuss things that are important to you professionally and how you plan to achieve them. If personal or professional growth is one of your goals, mention that. You can also talk about challenge, another value that employers prize in their employees:

- ☼ "I see myself working at a hospital that understands the importance of technology in documenting patient care."

- ☼ "In five years, I'd like to be chief financial officer." (Unless, of course, the hiring manager is the CFO. It's important to be diplomatic regarding your ambitions.)

- ☼ "My long-term goal is to create and manage the most successful sales team this company has ever had."

Keep in mind that most people couldn't possibly predict where they would be professionally five years from now. Nevertheless, this is a very popular interview question, so you should be prepared to answer it.

"Why Should We Hire You?"

When an interviewer asks you why she should hire you, speak confidently and directly about your abilities and how they will contribute to the company's bottom line—don't be afraid to blow your own horn. If you don't believe in yourself, who will?

- ☼ "I believe the combination of my project management skills and my master's degree in marketing make me an ideal candidate to help your company launch this new line of video games."

- ☼ "You mentioned that you would like to increase your sales of individual insurance policies for the twenty-two- to twenty-five-year-old college graduate. During my experience as an underwriter for Major Medical, Inc., I learned the needs of that demographic and can apply that knowledge to developing successful products for them."

Other standard questions that may come up are:

- ☼ What are the achievements you are most proud of?
- ☼ What is the most difficult situation you have faced and how did you handle it?
- ☼ Why have you applied for this job?
- ☼ Give me an example of a time you have worked under pressure.

Remember that the interviewer isn't interested in hearing that you "scored four touchdowns in one game" or that you applied for this job because you were "bored with your current position." Instead, he is trying to see if you have a good understanding of the job and what your role would be, how you would connect with the team, whether you are motivated by the work or the paycheck, and if you know your limits and can work around them.

INAPPROPRIATE INTERVIEW QUESTIONS

Inappropriate interview questions generally involve race, sex, religion, national origin, or age. Most interviewers will steer clear of these questions, but you'll want to guard against questions like these:

"How old are you?"
"Any plans to start a family?"
"What country are you from?"
"So, you got a boyfriend?"

Making a hiring decision based on the answers to these questions is at best poor practice and at worst illegal and, therefore, they should not come up in an interview. But, if they do, you have three options for handling them.

Answer the Question

If you don't strongly object to giving out the requested information, go ahead and do it so the interview can proceed. However, only do so if you are truly comfortable with this course of action. Otherwise, you're setting a precedent that you're accepting of inappropriate behavior.

Refuse to Answer the Question

Calmly tell the interviewer that the question doesn't seem relevant to the interview or the job's requirements. Save such a direct response, however, for questions that are truly offensive or deeply troubling—in other words, questions that bother you enough to make you reconsider taking the job.

Answer the Question *Behind* the Question

This is usually the best option, because it allows you to provide a tactful answer without sacrificing your rights. Try to figure out what the interviewer *really* wants to know.

For example, say an interviewer asks, even casually, your thoughts on having a family. What he really may be asking is if you plan to stay with the company for a long period of time. Instead of divulging personal information, say something like: "As with anyone else, of course family is important to me. However, what is most important to me right now is showing how I can help increase your bottom line by 20 percent."

Be careful what you divulge in an interview about your personal life, whether you are asked or not. If you plan to get married soon, are pregnant or soon to become pregnant, or have an illness or disability, you may not be obligated to mention this in an interview. If you have concerns or questions about inappropriate interview questions, visit the Equal Employment Opportunity Commission Web site at www.eeoc.gov.

THE TOUGHEST QUESTION OF ALL: "WHAT SALARY ARE YOU LOOKING FOR?"

Although salary may not come up in the first interview, sooner or later you will have that discussion—most likely with the recruiter. He may ask for your salary requirements, in which case you can give several answers—but *not* a hard number. Why? If your number is too low, you might get paid less than what you are worth (and what the company was willing to pay); too high and you can self-select yourself out of the running. Instead, give answers with ranges:

- ☼ "From my research I see that advertising firms in this region pay $50,000 to $60,000 for a position like this one."
- ☼ "I'd like to give this position some consideration first and perhaps call you with further questions. May we table this salary discussion until another time?"
- ☼ "What is the established range for this position?"

Another alternative is to give your salary range and, if they push back, say that you're open to discussing other forms of compensation (more vacation time, a signing bonus, stock options, and the like).

We'll discuss compensation further in chapter 9.

THINK Outside the Box

Five Ways to Rescue a Dying Interview

Sometimes interviews fizzle for no apparent reason. Here are some things you can do to get things back on track:

1. Smile. A big grin will help relax you and the interviewer.

2. Turn the tables. If you feel that you just aren't giving the right answers to an interviewer's questions, try changing tactics—and ask the interviewer a few questions of your own:

"What's your favorite thing about working here?"

"What's a typical day like working in this department?"

If you momentarily switch the focus from yourself to the interviewer, it will give you a chance to regroup and compose yourself. Also, it will make the interviewer do some talking, perhaps giving you a clue as to what she is looking for.

3. Ask for clarification. If your interviewer seems bored or confused by your answer to a question, stop and ask if you are giving her the information she's looking for.

4. Give a compliment. More specifically, give a compliment to the company. State how friendly everyone is or how nice the view is from the interviewer's window. This will show that you are a positive person without sounding insincere.

5. Do your best and move on. Maybe the discomfort is not your fault—maybe the interviewer is having a bad day or is just not that good at her job. Trust yourself and don't worry about things you can't control.

QUESTIONS OF YOUR OWN

You may feel that after the interviewer has asked his questions, you're in the clear. But you'll better your chances of being hired if you show that you have your own questions that go beyond "Where will I sit?"

For example:

- ☼ "In the next three months, what is the key task for the person filling this position?"
- ☼ "Can you tell me about the goals your department is expected to meet each year, and how that affects performance bonuses?"
- ☼ "What type of budget would I have to work with for these campaigns?"
- ☼ "PharmCorp was recently named one of *Pharmaceutical Monthly*'s Top 10 Companies to Watch. How do you think this department contributed to that success?"
- ☼ "Will I have the final say on new hires for my staff, or will they have to be approved by the executive board?"
- ☼ "How would you characterize your management style?"

You don't have to wait until the end of the interview for your own questions either—asking questions throughout makes the interview more of a mutual exchange than a one-way conversation.

NOW WHAT?

Waiting to hear the decision on a position is tough enough—don't leave a job interview without knowing the next step in the hiring process.

For example, will there be another round of interviews? When do they anticipate that a decision will be made? How quickly do they need someone to begin? When will you know the results? Not only will this information help reduce post-interview anxiety, it also shows the interviewer that you're thorough and conscientious.

THANK-YOU NOTES

However archaic they may seem, most career experts still recommend sending thank-you notes. Because so few job seekers do, if you send one, you'll likely stand out.

If you send a note, be prompt and professional. Handwritten notes are best; notes typed on paper and mailed are still good; but e-mail notes are becoming more acceptable. To make your note memorable, mention something specific about the interview—bring up an interesting fact or follow up on a trend you discussed. For example:

Dear Mr. Hayes,

Thank you for your time today. I truly feel that my experience as Sales Manager for Consolidated Corp. has given me the skills critical to leading your Widgets, Inc., sales team to success.

As I mentioned in our interview, by improving communication and implementing SalesHelper 2.0, I enabled the team I led at Consolidated to bring in 24 percent more business and come in $300,000 above our quota last year. I believe I can realize even higher returns for Widgets as your new Regional Sales Director.

I enjoyed meeting you and look forward to hearing from you soon.
Sincerely,
Jack Richards

SECOND AND THIRD INTERVIEWS

If the employer is interested and wants to know more about you, you'll be called back for a second or third interview (or maybe more). How will these be different from the first?

This time around, expect to spend more time at the company, talk to more people—possibly higher-level executives—individually and collectively, and have your skills and personality scrutinized more closely.

Before the interview, ask for a list of the people you'll be meeting with and their roles, and do a little research on each one. However, you may be surprised by who you meet. It may just be that the VP of marketing was available to ask a few questions or perhaps the hiring manager believes the IT director has an uncanny knack for reading people. As always, put your best foot forward, relax, and be yourself. Remember, they were once where you are sitting right now. They may ask questions for which you don't have the answer at hand, such as "How did the results of your campaign in Georgia compare to those in Wisconsin?" Don't be afraid to say you will get back to them. Your follow-through will give you one more chance to make a winning impression.

You may also be asked to give specific examples of ideas you would pitch to bring in more business and help the bottom line. At this level you'll be expected to demonstrate how your experience can benefit the new company.

Also, be aware that many employers bring in several candidates on the same day to streamline the second interview process. Your challenge is to distinguish yourself from the other candidates. You can do this by being up-to-date on the company's latest news, stock price, and the like, as well as by offering some unique ways your personality and skill set can help the company.

INTERVIEW ETIQUETTE

The way you come across in an interview will largely be unspoken. Your attire, punctuality (or lack thereof), and general demeanor may say more about you than your words.

Dress for Success

Even experienced job seekers struggle with what to wear to an interview. And today, as khakis and sneakers have pushed aside wool and linen in many work-places, it's easy to see why this would be confusing.

Professional attire, even if you are applying for a job that doesn't require it, is key. Why? Because your clothes give hints about who you are. Will a man who insists on wearing jeans while others are dressed in suits be a team player? Maybe so, but the clothes don't reflect that. Does a woman whose shirt doesn't match her skirt pay attention to details? Maybe, but unconsciously she's sending a message that she does not.

Interview attire can also have an effect on your salary offer. Research suggests that the right interview outfit can increase your salary between 8 and 20 percent, according to Susan Bixler, president of the corporate image consulting firm Professional Image, Inc. (www.professionalimageinc.com). An interviewer will believe that the way you look at the interview is the best you can do. What you wear makes a statement—so make it a good one.

- When deciding what to wear, err on the conservative side; also consider the company and the position. Don't wear excessive jewelry, makeup, perfume, or cologne. Men should wear a suit; women should wear a long skirt, pants, or a suit, and closed-toe shoes. Suits in conservative colors, such as black and navy, are a safe choice for both men and women. Both men and women should avoid casual shoes and "golf" shirts; turtlenecks are not advisable for men.

- Feel too stiff in a suit? Reconsider. In fact, Bixler recommends *always* wearing a jacket to interviews—this gives you a serious, professional appearance.

- Skirts more than one or two inches above the knee are an absolute no-no, as well as tight-fitting clothing, no matter how conservative.

- If you want to use your attire to express your individuality, do so in a *small, subtle* way. Women can wear a piece of tasteful jewelry, and men can sport an elegant tie.

Details Count

Now that you've figured out what to wear, here are some easier tips to remember:

Be ten to fifteen minutes early. Any more and you look overeager; any less and you are cutting it too close. Allow for traffic jams, the absence of parking spaces, and getting lost or otherwise delayed. Carry the recruiter's phone number with you in case you get unavoidably detained, and if you will be late, be sure to call and let him know.

Shake hands. A firm handshake is a must, whether you are a man or woman and whether the employer is a man or woman. A University of Alabama study found that a person's handshake reflects certain key personality traits, including confidence, degree of shyness, and neuroticism. (Not surprisingly, folks with firmer handshakes were found to be more confident, less shy, and less neurotic.) If sweaty hands are a problem, carry a tissue in your pocket to squeeze just before meeting someone.

Leave your cell phone off or in the car. This bears repeating. Leave your cell phone off or in the car.

What to Bring

You don't need the latest designer briefcase for an interview. But you *will* need:

- ☿ Several copies of your resume on quality paper. Don't assume that just because you have already e-mailed it to the employer she will have it— bring extras!

- ☿ Copies of your list of references. This list should consist of at least three people, be typed on a separate sheet of paper from your resume, and include the name, title, address, phone number, and e-mail address of each, if possible. Be sure to have your references' permission ahead of time and let them know when you think they may be called.

- ☿ Your personal portfolio, as discussed on page 128, including samples of your best work to share, if applicable.

- ☿ Business cards if you have them.

- ☿ A basic case, leather binder, or plain leather satchel to carry all these items.

- ☿ Finally, have everything at the ready. Scrounging through your purse for a pen is distracting.

THE WAITING GAME

By some estimates, the average job search takes as long as four to six months. Also, recruiters and hiring managers get detained with other duties. While their need to fill the position seemed immediate the day they interviewed you, maybe other issues have taken precedence since then.

If you don't hear anything, any number of other things could have happened. The hiring manager probably has other people to interview. He could have hired someone else or decided to hire internally. This is a common practice: A job is posted publicly (by law at some workplaces, such as government agencies), but a candidate within the company or government agency is promoted to the position.

Perhaps due to budget cutbacks or other internal changes, new hires have been pushed back to the next quarter. Maybe the company is undergoing reorganization or the hiring manager himself was laid off. Unfortunately, you won't know this unless the company contacts you—or you contact a company representative.

IS IT OK TO CALL?

Yes. But *within reason*. The day after you interview? No. After a week? Certainly, especially if the hiring manager was to give you a decision by that time.

If you are apprehensive about calling, e-mail can be less intrusive. Send a brief message such as, "Hello, I am following up on my interview with Ray Rogers on March 31. I enjoyed meeting all of you and was wondering if there is any other information I can provide you, or if you have made your decision."

The important point is, while you are waiting, keep searching! Don't stop sending out resumes, checking job postings, networking, and improving your resume and cover letters. Even if you are offered the job for which you inter-viewed, you may not like the compensation package, or you might find some-thing even better in the meantime. Never stop looking for the best job for you!

Congratulations—you're now prepared to clear the biggest hurdle in job seeking. No one likes interviews—and that includes the interviewer. Even long-time job seekers struggle with them. So know that you're not alone, and that you now have the tools to make this and every other interview in your future a success!

Recommended Books

Your Job Interview (Barnes & Noble Basics Series) by Cynthia Ingols (Silver Lining Books, 2003, ISBN 0760738556, $9.95).

Knock 'em Dead 2005: The Ultimate Job Seeker's Guide (Knock 'em Dead Series) by Martin Yate (Adams Media Corporation, 2004, ISBN 1593371063, $14.95).

101 Great Answers to the Toughest Interview Questions by Ron Fry (Thomson Delmar Learning, 2000, ISBN 156414464X, $11.99).

201 Best Questions to Ask on Your Interview by John Kador (The McGraw-Hill Companies, 2002, ISBN 0071387730, $12.95).

Sweaty Palms: The Neglected Art of Being Interviewed by H. Anthony Medley (Warner Business, 2005, ISBN 0446693839, $13.95).

Emily Post's Etiquette (17th ed.) by Peggy Post (HarperCollins Publishers, 2004, ISBN 0066209579, $39.95).

What Not to Wear: For Every Occasion by Trinny Woodall & Susannah Constantine (Riverhead Trade, 2004, ISBN 1594480508, $16.00).

QBQ! The Question Behind the Question: Practicing Personal Accountability in Work and in Life by John G. Miller (Penguin Group, 2004, ISBN 0399152334, $19.95).

Recommended Web Sites

Yahoo! HotJobs Interview Tips:
http://hotjobs.yahoo.com/interview

Equal Employment Opportunity Commission:
www.eeoc.gov

George Mason University Interviewing Strategies for Success:
http://careers.gmu.edu/students/jobhunt/interviewing.html

How to Interview:
www.howtointerview.com

The Professional Image—Article & Interview Archive:
www.theprofessionalimage.net/press.html

Salary.com Mock Job Interviews:
www.job-interview.net/sample/Demosamp.htm

CHAPTER 9

Your Paycheck...and Beyond: Salary and Benefits

*"There are no medical or pension benefits,
but the employees' lounge has excellent free coffee."*

By now you know that salary, while important, is only *part* of your overall compensation package. As an experienced worker, you are likely thinking more now about the future—your house, your family, your children's college tuition. A great salary is certainly the primary goal, but it's benefits like health care, pensions, and transit reimbursement that can make the difference in whether a company's offer is for you—or for you to dismiss.

Every worker has different needs when it comes to compensation. For example, a healthy, single, thirty-five-year-old woman might place more importance on salary and retirement benefits. But a married, thirty-five-year-old man with kids may put a premium on flex time, child care, and college savings accounts. The important thing is to evaluate the benefits that have the greatest impact on you and your lifestyle—and be sure to find those in your next job.

In this chapter, we'll examine salary and benefits, and what constitutes the right package for you and your family.

SALARY

Of course salary is important—everyone needs money. And to get the money you want, you'll need to keep the following in mind:

Home (in) on the Range

As you consider your next job, remember that salaries differ according to your experience, your education, the company's budget, whom the company hired for your department last week—any number of factors. Also, salaries vary depending on industry and region. In other words, the salary you could command at Company X in one industry in New England may be completely different from the one you could end up with at Company Y in another industry in New Mexico.

Unfortunately, you know little, if anything, about what a company is prepared to offer. For this reason, don't concentrate on a hard number, but come up with a range instead. Not only will this help you find a salary with which you and the employer are both comfortable, but it will also help when it comes time to negotiate. You're much more likely to successfully negotiate a good salary if you begin with a range than if you are rigid about a particular number.

What Are You Worth?

To understand what makes a good compensation package for you, you must first determine what salary range is commensurate with your experience level and skills for your chosen industry and location. There are several tools that can help you understand how salary varies across job titles and regions:

First, **Salary Wizard** lets you research salary by industry and location. Using this tool, you can find the average U.S. salary for a position or get more detailed information that takes your experience and employer into account. (See "Recommended Web Sites" at the end of this chapter.)

Yahoo! HotJobs Salary News also offers background on salaries for various industries as well as a "negotiation clinic."

We've discussed before the value of the **Occupational Outlook Handbook**. This handy book is also a helpful tool for researching salary information. Revised every two years, it includes up-to-date salary data on hundreds of jobs.

Visit the Web sites and directories of **professional associations**. Often they'll not only provide salaries for positions in a particular industry, but also ranges based on geographic location and experience level. Business- and industry-specific trade magazines and Web sites can offer insights too.

Finally, **use your network** to talk to people who work in the industry you're targeting. Salary is also a great subject for informational interviews. You don't have to ask anyone what they make specifically, but you can ask about trends and speak in generalities.

A *Smaller* Salary?

So far we've assumed that you are looking for a bigger and better salary with your new job, but you may be considering changing to a job that actually pays *less* than what you've been making—such as switching from management to creative or nonprofit work.

Although this outlook may sound grim, chances are if you're changing to a job you know you'll love, then salary becomes secondary. Of course, as we discussed in chapter 2, you may have to discuss this with your significant other or family first. You may have some very real considerations, like a mortgage or car payments, to keep in mind.

But a happier you is a healthier and more productive you, and you won't necessarily be in the red forever. In the meantime, there are ways to make up for the cut in pay, such as:

- ☼ Working part time on the side. Waiting tables, dog-walking, cleaning houses—you'd be surprised how pleasant these seemingly menial opportunities can be when you're living your life's dream from 9 to 5 each day.
- ☼ Freelancing, if you have the requisite skills and experience.

- ☼ Teaching or tutoring, leading seminars, or public speaking. Share your skill at candle making, fly-fishing, or anything you're good at that others would want to learn.

- ☼ Smart financial maneuvering: A financial adviser can show you how to capitalize on investments, real estate, interest rates, equity, and loans to fill in the gaps while you get your feet wet in your new job. (*Only* make such decisions with the advice of a trusted professional, and *never* look to credit cards as a solution.)

- ☼ Help from friends and family. This doesn't have to be monetary. It can be things as simple as child care, help around the house, and good old-fashioned emotional support.

- ☼ Simply cutting back. Eliminate coffeehouse lattes, magazine subscriptions, cable television, and the like.

A third of your life is spent at work, so you want to do something that truly speaks to your soul. If that means eating peanut butter and jelly for a while to save some money, so be it—you'll eventually get to where you want to be!

FAMILY BENEFITS

A standard job offer will include benefits worth a minimum of 25 percent or so of your base salary. And with all the benefits out there today, you'll have plenty to look for! Let's start with those benefits that pertain to family—even if you are single, or are coupled but don't have kids, a company's family benefits policies can still have an impact on you and your lifestyle.

Family and Medical Leave Act (FMLA)

Although this policy is not a benefit, but rather a federal mandate that most companies must abide by, you still should know its parameters, in case you ever need to use it.

The FMLA allows eligible employees of covered employers to take unpaid leave for up to twelve workweeks, due to:

- ☼ Birth/care of a child
- ☼ Placement of a child for adoptive or foster care
- ☼ Care for a seriously ill family member (spouse, parent, child)
- ☼ The employee's own serious health condition

Employees are entitled to return to their jobs or equivalent positions afterwards and keep their health benefits. Keep this policy in the back of your mind as an option in case of a major life event.

MATERNITY AND PATERNITY LEAVE

In actuality, *paid* maternity leave is uncommon in the United States. *Maternity leave* is simply the term for the time a mother takes off to care for a newborn or adopted child. *Paternity leave*, in which a *father* gets time off to care for a child, is even rarer and almost never paid. But the concept of paternity leave is growing in popularity.

Some companies offer limited paid time off—especially if you are a proven contributor or if you work for a small company that has more flexibility in its leave policies. Usually, though, parental time off is a combination of sick leave, short-term disability, FMLA, and other accrued leave, with the remainder unpaid.

But there is good news. You can work with a manager to extend your time or pay during family leave, according to Pat Katepoo, an adviser and family leave expert for Workoptions.com, a site for working parents seeking flexible work options.

"I encourage women to negotiate for more than what's offered in order to extend their time off with their new baby. Sometimes it's just a matter of asking coupled with a good work coverage plan," says Katepoo. "Your gut instinct is probably the best judge when deciding whether or not to make the request to be paid during leave. If you do, one to three weeks is a reasonable request—aim for that range."

Katepoo goes on to advise candidates to "check for signs that a prospective employer is family-friendly. At the interview, take note of how open employees are with signs of family life, such as photos on the desks and kids' artwork on the walls. This can be a reflection of employer culture and attitude. Do they have flexible work arrangements in place as an option for employees? Are they pro-moted and used? Do they have generous leave and/or vacation policies? Adoption subsidies? These are cues that the employer recognizes that their workforce has a life outside of their job."

So while maternity/paternity benefits are available at most companies, they have their limits. If you do find a compensation package that offers flexibility on time off or paid leave for new parents, and you plan to have a child in the near future, you would do well to consider that job.

take a memo

Not Just for Moms

Working Mother magazine's 100 Best Companies for Working Mothers is a great resource for finding companies with the best benefits packages. Even if you're not a mom, these companies are considered by many to offer the country's best all-around benefits. You can compare what you'll be getting from your new company to what these trailblazers offer.

Domestic Partner Benefits

Despite some controversy surrounding them, domestic partner (DP) benefits—health and dental insurance and other benefits for unmarried partners—are being offered at more and more workplaces. According to the Human Rights Campaign (HRC), a gay, lesbian, bisexual, and transgender organization, the number of colleges, governments, and private corporations offering documented DP benefits in 2005 numbered roughly 8,300. Laws regarding same-sex rights with respect to benefits are constantly changing. Know what you are entitled to.

If you are in a situation in which DP benefits could help you and your partner, you'll want to look for companies that offer them. (The HRC's database of employers that offer DP benefits is a great place to start: http://www.hrc.org.)

Be aware that domestic partner benefits, with some exceptions, can be taxed as income. It is also up to the company whether to offer DP benefits to same-sex partners, opposite-sex partners, or both.

Adoption Assistance

In an attempt to hold onto good employees and strengthen the fabric of society, some companies offer employees financial assistance to help offset the cost of adopting a child, which can run as high as $20,000 or more.

If adoption is something you're considering, this is a benefit you'll want to watch for.

Child Care and Elder Care

Whether it's an on-site child care facility or assistance toward paying for an outside facility or caregiver, child care is a benefit parents crave and companies offer to keep good employees. If a company does not have these benefits, take note if its culture is understanding of parental demands (such as pediatric appointments, teacher conferences, and soccer practice).

Meanwhile, even if you don't have children, America is aging—yet living longer than ever before. Elder care is fast becoming a concern for many workers with aging family members. Employers are beginning to accommodate this need with benefits such as leave policies and financial assistance in paying for care.

Here are some other benefits that can be of great help to workers caring for children or elders (and for the so-called "Sandwich Generation," caring for both at the same time):

- ☼ **Employee Assistance Programs (EAPs):** Counseling and resources for life events (see page 159).
- ☼ **Education and referral:** Seminars and resources for family care.
- ☼ **Employee networks:** Groups of employees who meet regularly to share information about dependent care (or other issues).
- ☼ **Flextime/compressed workweek:** Employee has flexibility in scheduling as long as weekly hour requirements are met.
- ☼ **Flexible spending arrangements:** Employees can set aside tax-free money for dependent care.
- ☼ **Daily details:** Unquestioned phone usage, lactation rooms, ability to bring children to work—little accommodations like these can be lifesavers for working parents.

In addition, some companies offer **compassion leave**. Full-time employees may voluntarily contribute personal leave hours or days to form a reservoir of additional paid personal leave for other employees confronted with an extended inability to work. Such inability may result from a catastrophic illness afflicting the employee, the employee's spouse, child, or parent. Keep in mind that a company that offers this kind of benefit usually has compassionate and family-friendly policies across the board.

RETIREMENT AND OTHER FINANCIAL BENEFITS

Another benefit you probably didn't give much thought to when you first entered the workforce is retirement benefits. While you still may be far from retirement age, you're smack in the middle of your life's period of greatest earning potential, so you want to make sure a good chunk of that money is being put aside for the future, and with your employer's help. As you interview for jobs, try to find positions with all or most of the following benefits.

401(k) Plans

You are probably already familiar with the 401(k) plan, and perhaps already have one. At this point in your career, the key in your next job is to make the most of your 401(k), and "catch up" if your previous retirement account took a big hit or if you've let your contributions slide. The best way to do this is to find a job with a company that allows you to put aside a percentage of your paycheck, and then matches a portion of your 401(k) contributions. Not all companies match your contribution, so this free money is something to consider as you evaluate a company's benefits.

Stock Options and Profit-Sharing

Stock options allow you to buy shares of a company at a future date with a set price. Stock options were especially popular during the Internet boom of the '90s. A handful of companies made even the most entry-level employees rich through stock options, but many people who chose them never saw a dime. Stock options, while risky, can mean a significant boost to your income at a successful company. But be very thorough in your research if stock options are a potential part of your compensation package, and don't count on them as part of your future income.

    Profit-sharing allows employees to earn a portion of a company's profits. Compensation can be in the form of cash, stocks, or bonds, and may be immediate or deferred.

Bonuses

Year-end bonuses can boost your bottom-line earnings because they generally come in the form of cold, hard cash. Year-end bonuses are typically awarded by profitable companies looking to share the wealth with employees. Know that you may have to be hired by a certain date (for example, before the beginning of the fourth quarter) in order to be eligible for these end-of-year bonanzas.

    Signing bonuses are one-time, instant cash payments for joining a company. You will, however, have to adhere to certain restrictions, such as working a minimum of one calendar year, as well as pay taxes on the bonus as regular income.

    Individual bonuses, on the other hand, are monies you receive based on your *personal* performance. These are common in careers such as sales. For example, a salesperson might receive a guaranteed 30 percent annual bonus for meeting specified goals—and this would be part of her compensation package. Again, these can be heavily taxed.

Pension Plans

Pension plans are funded by your employer and are *generally* guaranteed to provide a specific amount of money to you monthly after you retire. In most cases, even if a company goes bankrupt or runs into other financial trouble, organizations like the Pension Benefit Guaranty Corporation (PBGC) work to ensure you receive your pension, up to the limits set by law. (However, even the PBGC has struggled with historic losses in recent years.)

Once you're vested in the pension plan, that is, you've worked at the company long enough to become eligible to receive the pension when you retire, your pension is available to you upon retirement, no matter what your age when you began a job.

Larger companies and government jobs are more likely to offer pensions than smaller workplaces. However, pensions everywhere are becoming rarer, and even large companies have been struggling to meet their pension commitments.

"Pensions are disappearing, replaced by defined contribution plans such as 401(k)s that don't impact the company's balance sheet," says Peter Weddle, noted human resources expert and founder of consulting firm Weddle's. "Pension plans that continue are often seriously underfunded, but many employers are escaping through bankruptcy which transfers the obligation to the U.S. government (which is only obligated to pay pennies on the dollar to the pensioner)." According to the *Christian Science Monitor*, twenty years ago, 40 percent of American workers were covered by traditional pensions; today the number is around 20 percent.

What you get when you retire will be based on your salary and the number of years you worked for the company. Generally speaking, you become eligible for a pension after one year of service with a company, and you have to be vested for a minimum of three to five years before you qualify to *receive* your pension. Once you retire, you will get your pension whether you have worked at the company five years or thirty-five years. If you leave a job or retire early, you may have a variety of options, depending on the type of plan you have.

take a memo

Not So "United"

In mid-2005, facing bankruptcy, United Airlines found the fastest way to remedy its problems was to default on tens of thousands of pensions.

More worrisome was that the airline's problem was not unique. The steel industry had undergone similar traumas over the last twenty-five years, the auto industry was potentially facing pension problems, and even the Pension Benefit Guaranty Corporation, the organization that was supposed to ensure the United pensions in case of default, was facing its largest losses in history.

Strangely, one group of people walked away from the United debacle unscathed: United's pension *advisers*, who collected more than $125 million in fees in the five years leading up to the scandal. (Mary Williams Walsh, "How Wall Street Wrecked United's Pension," *New York Times*, July 31, 2005.)

HEALTH CARE

By now you've probably had at least one medical incident in your life that made you glad that you had health insurance (or wish you had). Despite its rising costs in recent years, having health coverage is critical both for you and for your family.

Most companies today offer several health care plan options. Unlike when you were first entering the workforce and could get by with basic coverage, the key now is to pick the plan that best fits the needs of you and your family—and your budget, as you will likely have to contribute part of your paycheck toward coverage.

Previously you may have used an HMO, but perhaps you want access to more specialists with a Preferred Provider Organization (PPO) in your next job. While you may not have used vision coverage in the past, this benefit could be more important now that you are considering getting contacts. Mental health and substance abuse counseling, as well as alternative health care treatments (massage, acupuncture, and the like) might also be something of greater value to you now. Or simply for the sake of practicality, if one company offers the same insurance plan you currently have, but another offers different options and your current doctor is not in the network, you may lean toward the first company.

You'll have to do a line-by-line comparison of plans at potential new jobs to see which are best for your circumstances. No matter what your health care options, the most critical question for each component is this: *When do they take effect?* In some companies, you're covered the day you walk in the door. At others, there's a ninety-day waiting period. If you're considering multiple employment offers, this could be a deciding factor in choosing one job over another.

FLEXIBLE SPENDING ACCOUNTS (FSAs)

These convenient plans are another great perk you'll want to watch for. FSAs allow you to put money aside tax free for medical expenses not covered by your health care plan. These costs include such things as co-pays, prescription costs, or lasik eye surgery if your employer does not offer a vision plan.

Flexible spending accounts can pay off during years in which you anticipate a lot of medical, dental, or vision expenses that will not be covered by insurance. Make sure you understand what the FSA will cover and the conditions for reimbursement.

Most FSAs require a receipt and require you to file your expenses by a given deadline; usually you cannot carry over the balance into the next year. So you have to make your claims or you lose your money.

OTHER IMPORTANT BENEFITS

Now let's discuss some other important benefits that you might not have considered as thoroughly in the past.

Dental and Vision

Sure you had 20/20 vision when you were twenty, but now you may find yourself struggling to read those PowerPoint presentations. And even if your teeth are perfect, what if the twins need braces in a few years? Dental and vision coverage vary from company to company. For example, some vision plans cover contacts and glasses, others just the exam. And smaller companies might not offer these benefits at all. So be sure to look for these important offerings as you study companies' benefits plans.

Life Insurance, Short-term Disability (STD), Long-term Disability (LTD), Worker's Compensation

These benefits replace some (but not necessarily all) lost income in the event of death or an illness that prevents the employee from working. You may not be worried about your health, but you now may have more people counting on you—be sure that you have enough coverage for them, and that they know your wishes and how to access these benefits.

hot facts

Did You Know...?

According to the Insurance Information Institute, at age forty, the average worker faces only a 14 percent chance of dying before age sixty-five—but a 21 percent chance of being disabled for ninety days or more.

Long-Term Care

Although not yet a standard benefit, companies are beginning to offer long-term care insurance (usually for an additional employee contribution) as a way of ensuring the employee's lifestyle in the event of a catastrophic and *ongoing* illness, or a serious accident. As opposed to LTD coverage, long-term care applies to those who can no longer work or perform daily tasks by themselves, and require care in their home or in an assisted-living facility or nursing home.

College Savings Assistance

Little Janie may only be three, but it's never too early to start thinking about paying for her college education. College savings plans allow you to set aside money, with tax advantages, to save or invest for college tuition. (By the way, every state has a version of a college savings program, so you can open an independent account if your new employer doesn't offer this benefit.)

Time Off

This includes vacation days, personal days, sick days, and holidays. Don't just look at the number of days allotted per year. Consider when you can start taking advantage of them. How many years of employment until your vacation time (or sick leave) increases? Is it possible to "roll over" any unused days into the next year? Are there "floating holidays" to make up for situations in which you will be called upon to work on national or religious holidays?

Education/Training

If a company offers ongoing training in computers, negotiation, public speaking, or other skills, not only will this help to advance your career, but you can use these skills outside of work, too. So that's definitely a benefit worth considering.

Tuition Reimbursement

We discussed the value of tuition reimbursement programs in chapter 2. Look for this benefit—especially if you expect to pursue further schooling. This benefit can save you thousands of dollars and help promote your career.

Transportation Savings Programs

Companies use transportation programs to help employees reduce their commuting costs. The currency for many of these programs is the transit (or commuter) check, redeemable for public transportation, including buses, subways, and trains. Some companies also cover parking fees.

These programs save employees money by buying transit checks with pre-tax dollars. Specifically, the company deducts the amount of the transit check from an employee's paycheck before taxes are deducted.

Employee Assistance Programs

An Employee Assistance Program (EAP) is a counseling and referral program. Employers pay for these programs, so what could be costly professional care is provided free to their workers. Employee Assistance Programs can help you with a wide array of personal, financial, and health care concerns:

- Child and elder care
- Credit, financial, and tax issues
- Legal issues
- Mental health counseling
- Parenting skills
- Substance abuse

Most programs offer a toll-free hotline for assistance. If you prefer a face-to-face meeting, many will also provide referrals to professionals in your area. Many of these programs provide confidential emergency counseling around the clock.

Employee Networks

These are groups of employees with common interests (child care, elder care) or backgrounds (race, ethnic heritage) who hold regular meetings and events. They provide resources and support, and can also help you learn about job openings or find references—a great way to expand your own network. These groups are often "sponsored" by executives, giving employees informal "face time" with higher-ups they might not normally encounter.

Where salary and benefits are concerned, only you know what's most important for you and your family. Whether your priorities are a top-notch salary and stock options or just someone to walk Fido once in a while, the salary and benefits package should make your life easier and happier. Research thoroughly, have the necessary discussions with friends and family, and then seek jobs that match your needs—they're out there. In the next chapter, we'll show you what to do when you are offered one.

Recommended Books

401(k)s for Dummies by Ted Benna & Brenda Watson Newmann (John Wiley & Sons, Inc., 2002, ISBN 0764554689, $16.99).

Retire on Less Than You Think: The New York Times Guide to Planning Your Financial Future by Fred Brock (Henry Holt & Company, Inc., 2004, ISBN 0805073744, $15.00).

The Wall Street Journal Guide to Understanding Personal Finance by Kenneth M. Morris & Virginia B. Morris (Simon & Schuster, 2004, ISBN 0743266323, $15.95).

Recommended Web Sites

Yahoo! HotJobs Salary & Benefits:
http://hotjobs.yahoo.com/salary

Yahoo! HotJobs Salary Wizard:
http://hotjobs.salary.com

Yahoo! HotJobs Salary News:
http://hotjobs.com/salarynews

Yahoo! Health—Health Insurance Guide:
http://health.yahoo.com/health/centers/insurance

U.S. Department of Labor's Statistics on Wages, Earnings, and Benefits:
www.bls.gov/bls/wages.htm

Assurant Health—Insurance company specializing in individuals and those between jobs:
www.assurantdirect.com

***Fortune*'s 100 Best Companies to Work for:**
http://www.fortune.com/fortune/bestcompanies

***Working Mother* Magazine:**
www.workingmother.com

Max Maternity Leave Proposal (from Workoptions.com):
http://www.workoptions.com

Sealing the Deal: Negotiating and Accepting the Offer

"Stock options won't do it. I'll also need a ball of yarn."

At last, after all the worry, the late nights searching, the writing and rewriting of countless resumes and cover letters, you finally have a job offer! But as you probably know by now, starting a new job isn't just about showing up and claiming a cubicle.

For one thing, the offer is only the beginning. When you first entered the workforce, you didn't have much leverage and pretty much took what you could get. Now not only do you bring more to the table, but you need and *deserve* a compensation package that rewards your skills and accomplishments and supports you and your family. So you need to look for ways to finesse the offer to your liking through the delicate art of negotiation.

Also, as a midcareer professional quite possibly departing from another job, you still have some important decisions and paperwork to sort out before you begin the next one. In this chapter we'll examine some of the final steps you'll need to take before moving on to your dream job.

Negotiating

As the saying goes, "Everything is negotiable." Most employers at your level will, in fact, expect a little pushback from you once you receive the offer. So relax—no one's the "bad guy" here. Rather than a confrontation, a good negotiation actually is a back-and-forth that eventually should achieve common ground with which both parties are satisfied.

Depending on your age, previous jobs, and comfort level with confronting others, you may have little if any negotiating experience. Or perhaps you have tried negotiating unsuccessfully before and want to improve your chances for the next time. So what can you expect from a negotiation at this stage in your career? What are the best strategies for getting what you want? Where do you make a stand and where do you back down?

Come Prepared

First, be confident in your research, and in *yourself*. You deserve a great compensation package—and you have the accomplishments to back that up.

Second, have those accomplishments close at hand. Keep your top successes in mind as you enter a negotiation, just as you did in the interview. Being able to reiterate exactly how you can help the company just might be the little push the hiring manager needs to give you that extra $2,000 in salary.

You've done your homework regarding realistic salary ranges by visiting salary Web sites and talking to people in the industry. If you feel that the offer the company made is not on par with the industry standard, you can respond by saying something like this:

As I've considered this wonderful opportunity and researched others like it, I've found that the salary range tends to fall more in the $XX range. I understand that different companies have different policies for salary. Can you tell me why this one falls into the lower range?

Or,

As you know, I have eight years' experience in snack food packaging and recently won the regional Golden Pretzel award for packaging design. I feel these accomplishments warrant a slightly higher compensation package. I sense that I'd be very happy here, however. What can we do to find some middle ground?

Or,

To be honest, the salary isn't quite what I was looking for, but I understand your benefits here are top-notch. Can you tell me more about those and then can we get back to salary?

All of these are polite, open-ended, yet direct statements that show you are up on your industry research. They also put the onus on the employer to explain and defend the offer further. Finally, all compliment the employer but subtly suggest that the offer is not yet where you would like it to be, and you will not say yes until you get a higher offer, more benefits, or at least a reasonable explanation.

Recognize Limitations

Although there is usually some wiggle room in an offer, hiring managers have limitations beyond their control. For one thing, hiring managers have budgets to consider, and they may not even have much say in what those are.

They also have to keep things fair for your peers—positions will generally have set salary ranges so that Sally isn't making more than Sam for the same work, and to allow for raises as you grow in your job.

So while it's fine to ask for more, if you sense that an employer's hands are tied, or you're applying for a position such as government work or teaching (in which you're most likely to get the going rate for public institutions with pre-established salary scales), you're probably going to have to accept the offer as is. Fortunately, your research should alert you to these types of salary limits before you enter the negotiation.

Think Flexibility

Even if you are pleased with the salary offer, there are still benefits to consider—remember that salary is only part of the package! A great salary won't matter much if you need domestic partner benefits and the company doesn't offer them, or if you had five weeks' vacation in your previous job and only get two with this new company.

So memorize this question: Is there any flexibility here? Asking about "flexibility" is a tactful way of seeing if you can get more—more money, more vacation time, more anything. You won't seem pushy or greedy; rather, you will seem calm, professional, and prepared—exactly the sort of person they want to have working there.

Here are some sample situations in which inquiring about flexibility gives the job seeker an advantage:

HR Rep: *Hello Ms. Adams. This is David Simms with Propane USA. I'm calling to let you know that we are extending you an offer to join our regional sales staff.*

You: *Thank you. I'm very pleased to receive the offer.*

HR Rep: *We're prepared to offer you a $67,000 base salary, with commission and full benefits.*

You: *Thank you. Is there any flexibility in the salary? Considering my five years' experience as sales director with Grills-R-Us, and my familiarity with hazardous materials, I'd like to aim more toward the $72,000–75,000 range.*

HR Rep: *Unfortunately, due to budget restrictions, the salary is non-negotiable.*

You: *I see. Are benefits negotiable? I currently have four weeks' vacation time, and I'd like to talk about adding more time to your standard two weeks for new employees.*

HR Rep: *I think that, given your level of qualifications, we can consider additional vacation time. We also have a Performance Plus program that allots money each quarter as an incentive for high performers. Normally you have to be employed with us for a year before you're eligible, but I think we can make an exception here. Why don't I discuss some options with the hiring manager and then we can speak about this further on Wednesday?*

You: *Thank you. I appreciate your flexibility.*

Another possibility:

HR Rep: *Hello Mr. Davis. This is Samantha with Happy Days Greeting Cards. I'm calling to invite you aboard as our new office manager.*

You: *Wonderful! I'm very happy to hear that!*

HR Rep: *We're prepared to offer you a starting salary of $48,000 plus benefits.*

You: *Thank you for the offer. But considering my fluency with the latest desktop publishing programs, my experience in training, and my leadership of the office of the CEO for a Fortune 500 company, I was hoping for a starting salary in the $55,000–60,000 range. Is that possible?*

HR Rep: *We like to try and leave some room in starting salaries for growth. However, considering that you do have a level of experience that compares with some of our top employees, we can adjust the salary to $54,000.*

You: *Would you be open to $55,000 now with a review after six months and the possibility of an increase then?*

HR Rep: *I can certainly speak with the hiring manager about that and see what we can do.*

You: *Thank you. I'm very excited about the offer, and I look forward to hearing back from you about this final point.*

These examples were abbreviated, of course, and in real life might take place over several days with some involvement by the hiring manager. But in both of these situations, both sides were polite and upfront about their needs. In both, the job seekers looked for additional ways to increase their compensation package, *and* were willing to give some thought to the matter first.

You might just get your dream offer the first time around, and if you do, by all means go ahead and take it. Otherwise, you should always be looking for ways to improve the offer—showing company representatives that you're the smart, confident employee they want on their team.

THINK Outside the Box

Six Extra Benefits

In lieu of a higher salary, consider asking for:

1. **More vacation time.** This gives you more paid free time, but it's "soft dollars" to employers and its cost is less overt.

2. **A title change.** Changing a title from "account manager" to "account executive" costs your employer nothing, but can be a boost for your resume.

3. **Tuition assistance.** If your company doesn't offer it, ask if they might explore that for you. If they do offer it, see if you can squeeze an extra class or two out of them.

4. **Telecommuting.** Perks like telecommuting, flextime, and compressed workweeks are becoming much more common and accepted in today's global economy. Ask if it's possible for you—thereby saving you time and commuting costs.

5. **Midyear salary review.** You might get your employer to agree to a salary review and raise, should you be exceeding your goals, after six months (be certain to get this perk in writing).

6. **Relocation expenses.** If you're moving across the country or even just across town, ask if the company will pay all or part of your moving expenses.

Title Trials

Sometimes, there's just nothing like handing out that business card with the title "Empress of All She Surveys" on it—or at least "Manager." Different companies have different structures for job titles, and they're not necessarily tied to salary. Yet to many a title can be a sticking point in negotiations. If you're used to being an "Account Executive" at one company, you might not want to take the title of "Account Manager" at another, even if the job is exactly the same.

As with salary budgets, at large companies titles are often tied to company hierarchy charts and can be tough to change—especially if more than one person holds that title. However, it's always worth trying. And if you are applying for a job at a smaller company, you may have more flexibility.

Consider how important a job title is to you, and come up with some reasonable suggestions of your own to offer. But in the end, it's the salary

and benefits that appear on your paystub—not the title on your business card—
that should count.

How Far Do You Push?

There is value in negotiating, but you don't want to go overboard. If you keep
pushing for more and more, you might lose your chance at the job. At best,
you'll annoy your new employer and start your new relationship off on the
wrong foot. Only push hard for the things you truly want and need—things that,
should you not get them, will allow you to freely walk away from the offer and
feel good about doing so.

However, you don't want to settle for an offer that doesn't meet your needs,
or accept too quickly because you're scared of angering the employer. Take
the example of Jake, a Web developer. When offered a full-time job from a
company for which he had been contracting, Jake was thrilled. He'd made
friends there, knew the products well, and enjoyed going to work every day.
He was, in fact, so ready to have a steady, full-time job again that as soon as
the offer was made, he said yes on the spot, even though he had hoped for
$5,000 more in salary. He didn't want to run the risk that his boss would change
his mind.

Jake worked hard the next four months, through a staff reorganization and
the launches of three major products. But when it was time for annual raises
and bonuses, he discovered that he didn't qualify because he'd been hired too
late in the previous year. It would be another full calendar year before he was
eligible. But what bothered him the most was the knowledge that had he asked
for his original desired salary, the unavailability of a bonus wouldn't have mat-
tered. He'd already have gotten the money he wanted.

Decide ahead of time what you absolutely need in your job, salary- and
benefit-wise. Also consider the less tangible opportunities and perks—training
classes, leadership opportunities, commute, and casual dress—those things
that will make your life easier and help you build your resume for your next job.
A job that pays $2,000 less than another, but is thirty minutes closer to your
home and offers free training classes, sounds like a job well worth taking.

One last issue—we've discussed negotiating under the assumption that the
hiring manager is willing to work with you. But you may find that a manager is
inexplicably rigid and inflexible in his offer, despite your research to the contrary.
If a manager says "no" to your requests, politely inquire as to why. If the answer
is something along the lines of "take it or leave it," then the company may not be
the best place for you.

take a memo

Negotiating Dos and Don'ts

- ☼ Don't say yes right off the bat—take at least a day or two to think about the offer.
- ☼ Do use research in considering your offer, but . . .
- ☼ Don't hand out the printouts of salary comparisons to your potential employer.
- ☼ Don't negotiate just for the sake of negotiating—once you reach a deal you're happy with, accept it.
- ☼ Do be confident in your demands, but . . .
- ☼ Don't be greedy.
- ☼ Do be flexible.
- ☼ Do consider asking for flexibility in benefits—more vacation time, telecommuting, or tuition assistance.

THEY LIKE YOU, THEY *REALLY* LIKE YOU!

You're ready, once again, to pack up the briefcase and rejoin your fellow workers in a job that will, hopefully, be closer to what you want and provide greater fulfillment—until, of course, the time comes to change again (and it almost certainly will).

However, there are a few final hurdles to negotiate. First, you need to officially accept the offer—or choose between offers if you've received more than one. Then, you have to present the situation to your boss. Finally, there are some etiquette issues and some paperwork with which you may be unfamiliar, especially if you haven't changed jobs in a while.

Want the Job? Don't Wait

Employers understand you will need to think about an offer. Most employers will be reasonable, and won't expect you to get back to them the next day. However, don't think about it for too long. A few days is acceptable while you consider your decision, so give them an exact date that you'll get back to them with a decision, and do it. In the meantime, even if you have just been offered the job of your dreams, this is a good time to pause and consider your next move.

Continue to be respectful, professional, and polite in your conversations with company representatives—don't make the mistake of thinking that, once you have an offer, you no longer need to be on your best behavior.

Juggling Offers

Because you have so many talents and skills, it's not beyond the realm of possibility that you might get not one, but two or more job offers at once. While this can be an ego boost the size of the Pacific Ocean, it can also be extremely stressful.

Each job will have its pros and cons, of course. You will need to take a close look at the impact of each one on your career path, family, commute, and the like to determine which job is the right choice. Consider the following:

- ☼ Look closely at what is being offered. Compare the salary and benefits. Do the jobs give you and your family the best in support and security? How do the commutes compare? Does one allow for a more flexible schedule than the other?

- ☼ Is one riskier, such as a start-up or a company that has just laid off four hundred workers, while the other appears more solid?

- ☼ Consider upward mobility. Does one allow opportunity for greater—or faster—advancement? Is one a better match for where you ultimately want to go in life?

- ☼ Consider the management styles of your would-be supervisors. Could you picture yourself having a more autonomous roll working for one manager than another? Is one's management style more compatible with your preferred way of working?

- ☼ Will one of the jobs require relocation, and if so, will the company offer assistance?

- ☼ While everyone will have a learning curve in a new job, do you feel more confident about your abilities in one job compared to the other?

- ☼ Does one company place more emphasis on the community and environ-ment than the other (i.e., community service days or recycling programs)?

- ☼ Sit down and imagine accepting one job and think through where your life might be a few years down the road. Do you like the image? Try out the other job in your imagination. How would your life be then?

- ☼ Will one or the other simply make you happier on a daily basis?

Questions like these still may not produce the perfect answer. However, it's not the end of the world to have two great offers from which to choose. With thought and research, you can't make a "wrong" choice. And as we discussed in chapter 1, the day will come when you'll change jobs again—you likely won't be in this new job forever, so make your choice with the information you have and get going!

Counteroffers

You've made up your mind which job you want—let the celebration begin, right? Not necessarily. Just when you decline one company's offer, the recruiter may come back with a counteroffer—an increase in the original salary and/or benefits package. Or perhaps your current company tries to keep you on by matching or bettering the offer you received. And suddenly you're back at square one.

First, realize that this is a positive situation. Clearly, two companies appreciate your value and are willing to work with you to make you happy. This also puts you in the driver's seat for getting what you want (within reason).

Second, consider again what's important to you. Remember, just because the salary offer has increased for one job, that doesn't suddenly make that job's long commute any easier. Remember why you opted for the other job in the first place—does this new competing offer make the job more attractive, or is it just the dollar signs you see?

If it's your *current* job that makes the counteroffer, ask yourself why you wanted to leave—will those reasons change with a heftier paycheck? Many industry experts say no, and recommend declining a counteroffer from the company where you're currently working because it creates confusion about your worth: If a company is willing to pay you 20 percent more now, why weren't they doing that in the first place? Will you still be considered as valuable later on, when the dust settles? Will you be suspected of job searching every time you take a day off? Will your current company secretly begin to seek to replace you with a lower-salaried employee? And will your peers still accept you after you had one foot out the door?

To handle a counteroffer, continue to be professional. If you receive a counteroffer but still prefer the first offer, you're in the clear—accept the first job and decline the second in a reasonable amount of time.

If you prefer the counteroffer, accept it and let the other company know immediately that you are out of the running for the position that was offered to you.

Or, you can take a big risk. The third possibility is trickier: You can use the counteroffer to negotiate a better deal from the company you prefer. This is a perfectly acceptable practice—this is business, after all, and you should try to get yourself the best compensation possible. But exercise extreme caution and avoid giving an ultimatum.

Tell the first company that you have received a counteroffer. You do not have to disclose salary details. Just as you did when you first entered negotiations, state what you would like them to give you to "up the ante," or ask if there are any points on which they are flexible. If the answer is no, you'll need to decide if their offer is still good enough for you in light of the counteroffer.

If the answer is yes, then work with the hiring manager to settle on final terms, and let the other company know immediately that you are declining to work there, despite their generous counteroffer.

Don't be overconfident and try to pull the companies into a bidding war. Even if you get what you want, you risk leaving a bad taste in the companies' mouths. Also, don't bluff and say you have a competing offer when you don't. This is extremely risky, and you'll be in quite a bind if the recruiter says he can't match your invented offer.

IT'S NOT YOU, IT'S ME...

Turning down an offer without turning off the hiring manager takes great skill. You want the hiring manager to respect and remember you in the future—especially if you really liked that particular company. You never know when that same company may launch a whole new division with better-fitting opportunities. Or, for whatever reason, the job you decide to take may not turn out to be what you expected.

Call the recruiter—not the hiring manager—with your news, and within the decision time you specified. Do not decline an offer by e-mail. This shows that you didn't care enough about their offer to do more than type out a few sentences.

Say that you've given their offer "much consideration." While you are "honored" that they would select you, you have decided not to accept the job at this time.

Depending on your reason for declining, you might even ask that they keep your resume on file—especially in cases where you liked the company, but were lukewarm about the job itself.

Here are some ideas about what you can say:

☼ "I don't feel this position is the right fit for me at this time."

☼ "After much thought, I feel my skills would be better utilized in XYZ capacity. Please keep my resume on file if that position becomes available."

☼ "I feel that in order to achieve my goal of obtaining a position in marketing, I should focus my search there."

If you have taken a job with another company, you do not need to offer that information—especially if it's with a competitor. Just be businesslike and thank the recruiter for her time.

MAKING IT OFFICIAL

Accepting a new job is a joyous occasion, and once you've made your decision, you're probably ready to hit the ground running. But, as you know, first there is some important paperwork involved, not to mention properly extracting yourself from your current job, if you have one.

Setting a Start Date

Setting a start date can be frustrating. You want to start off your new job on the right foot, but you also want and need some time to tie up loose ends. Your new employer may suggest a date for you, but before you agree (and this may even come up in negotiations before the offer is finalized), consider things such as:

☼ **Ongoing and upcoming projects at your current job.** What projects are you involved in and how long will it take to successfully complete or transition them to another teammate? Are there big projects coming down the pike you would be expected to help with or lead?

☼ **Accrued sick and vacation time.** Whatever personal leave you have stored up, take it before you leave the job—it's yours. Also be aware of your "vesting" time for benefits like pensions and 401(k). You wouldn't want to leave two weeks before those monies became yours.

☼ **Family and personal time.** Remember those people in your house every night? You may want to allow for some downtime with them or a vacation before starting a new position.

☼ **Relocation.** Obviously, moving, whether assisted by the new job or not, is a major stressor. Allow plenty of time to find a new place, pack and move, and settle in. Also consider that moving companies aren't always on schedule with delivery of your goods.

You will need, of course, to give your current employer the standard two weeks' notice, and you may need additional time on top of that. Work with the new employer to establish a start date that you're both comfortable with. If they need you sooner than you can go, suggest starting on a part-time basis so you can meet all your commitments.

Employers generally understand that you have many things to attend to before you start a new job, and they are usually willing to wait. After all, they hope that one day, if you leave, you'll show them the same respect.

Telling Your Manager

Now comes another tough situation (unless you're ecstatic to leave, of course): telling your manager the news.

The emphasis here is on telling your manager, in person, that you are leaving. Not by phone, or e-mail, but face to face. No matter how much you may dislike your job or your manager, you still need to take the time to have a face-to-face conversation about your departure. Also, be sure that your manager hears the news from you first—don't tell others at work lest someone slip up and tell your manager before you do.

You do not need to explain why you are leaving, unless you choose to do so. (Often your HR department will have you undergo an "exit interview" process in which you can disclose further details, if you like.) You certainly do not need to discuss your new compensation package. If anything, be positive, stating that you feel you have more opportunities for growth with the new position, and assure your boss that you will be sure to wrap up all outstanding tasks before you leave. No matter what your relationship with your manager or company, you want to leave on good terms.

Coaching Your Coworkers

It's likely before you leave that your coworkers are going to need some help taking over your tasks. It may be tempting to leave everyone at work in the lurch—especially if you feel you've been mistreated at your current job. But do your best to be positive and helpful until it's time to go. Don't leave the worker filling your place stuck trying to figure out your filing system or searching your computer for where you stored that important contract. It's (probably) not Renée's fault you are leaving, so don't punish her. Departing without helping your coworkers with the transition will leave a bad impression—something that could come back to haunt you someday—and, frankly, just isn't very kind or mature.

In addition, stay focused on your current job those last few weeks. Now is not the time to start slacking off because you know you're leaving. Stay on task, and keep the calls to moving companies and your new manager to a minimum. You are still on your current company's payroll.

Paperwork

Your new job will require you to fill out plenty of paperwork—dealing with everything from bank accounts to beneficiaries—before you are officially employed. Let's review some of the most important ones.

Offer Letter

While most job offers will be given verbally, either at the end of a second interview or over the phone, you should always make sure you get the offer in writing, in the form of the offer letter. (Be extremely wary of any company that won't put their offer in writing.)

The offer letter protects you and your prospective employer by stating in writing what you both expect to happen upon your hiring, such as:

- ☼ The exact position you are being offered
- ☼ Your start date
- ☼ Your eligibility for performance bonuses
- ☼ Your salary
- ☼ Pay periods the company uses (twice a month, every two weeks, every week, and so on)
- ☼ The benefits package you're entitled to
- ☼ Your supervisor

You might also ask if there is a written job description that could be attached to the job offer letter, again so that both you and your new employer know what to expect. Be warned, however, that the formal offer will be contingent on you passing whatever other tests might be left (see page 176).

Contract

Similar to the offer letter, an "employment contract" is a more formal (and probably lengthier) legal document that states the rights, obligations, and expectations of the company and the employee. If your job offer includes an employment contract, be sure to take the time to read it carefully and consult an attorney if you have any questions.

Noncompetes

You might be asked to sign a noncompete agreement that prohibits you from working in the same field for a length of time after you leave your new job. You will probably need to sign it as a condition of employment, but if you don't feel comfortable signing it, ask for an attorney's advice. Keep in mind that this could severely limit your employment options for a period of time if things don't work out and you want to seek a similar job with a different employer.

Nondisclosure Agreements

A nondisclosure agreement (NDA)—also known as a "confidentiality agreement" or "confidential disclosure"—is a contract between you and the company stating that you will not divulge company information to *anyone*. NDAs are standard in many industries in which information and business practices are closely guarded. If it is a condition of employment, you will need to sign it, but, again, seek out the advice of an attorney if you don't understand the implications of this document or if you feel uncomfortable about signing it.

HR Forms

Health care, life insurance, payroll, 401(k)—if you don't get your benefits forms signed and submitted on time, these important elements of your compensation may be delayed. You do not want to miss enrolling in a health care plan and have to wait until the following quarter to sign up, or miss out on a month's worth of company 401(k) matching funds because you lost the form. Same goes for des-ignating investment and insurance beneficiaries. These are small but important details to take care of as soon as possible, especially if you have a family. The best idea? Block off a few hours on your calendar and get all your personal paperwork done before orientation, training classes, and lunches with new coworkers fill up your schedule.

Some Paperwork of Your Own

You've received a letter formalizing the job offer; now, you might respond with a letter of your own, accepting the offer. It's a nice touch, from a professional standpoint, and gives you the chance to put in writing what you understand the scope of the job to be.

What should you say in your acceptance letter? Once again, be as profes-sional as possible and restate what you understand to be the job title and major responsibilities, salary and benefits package, and your starting date.

And as long as you are in the letter-writing mode, why not keep going and send out letters (or at least e-mails) to the people who've helped you in your job search? This is the perfect time to thank them for their help, inform them of your success, and let them know that you won't forget them as you pursue your career. Send a note of thanks that includes the news of your new job to:

- ☼ Former coworkers and managers (if you feel comfortable doing this)
- ☼ Human resources staff at your old and new companies
- ☼ Networking contacts and mentors
- ☼ Former clients (provided a noncompete does not limit your contact with them)

OTHER ODDS AND ENDS (THAT MAY SEEM ODD)

Often today, job offers are contingent on some important, and perhaps slightly worrisome, "tests." However, drug tests and credit and background checks are common and legal.

Drug Tests

Depending on the position you've applied for and the company culture, you may be asked to take a drug test. While an employer can't force you to take one, if you refuse, you probably will no longer be considered for employment. If a drug test is required, the recruiter will give you the necessary information, but setting up the appointment will likely be your responsibility.

Credit Checks

When you first applied for the job, you may have signed a piece of paper giving the recruiter permission to run a credit check on you. By now you may be well-acquainted with credit checks from having bought a car or a house. Your potential employer also has an interest in your credit history. It may seem unfair, but companies will have doubts about hiring someone who has made repeated bad financial decisions in her personal life, especially if she will be handling a budget.

Background Checks

Finally, when you applied for the job, you may have signed a form granting company representatives permission to perform a background check on you. Background checks search items like previous addresses, college and work history, and whether you have a criminal record. They are performed by outside agencies.

OFF AND RUNNING

Congratulations! Not only have you received a job offer (or several), but you've successfully negotiated a great compensation package, accepted the offer, and completed every last detail of paperwork. Good for you!

Now we'll offer just a few more final tips as you begin the next chapter of your career journey, to help you start off on the right foot and make your transition as smooth as possible.

Recommended Books

Getting to Yes: Negotiating Agreement Without Giving In by Roger Fisher & William Ury (Penguin, 1991, ISBN 0140157352, $15.00).

The Art of Negotiating by Gerard I. Nierenberg (Barnes & Noble Books, 1995, ISBN 156619816X, $5.98).

Get Paid What You're Worth: The Expert Negotiators' Guide to Salary and Compensation by Robin Pinkley & Gregory Northcraft (St. Martin's Press, 2000, ISBN 0312242549, $23.95).

The Good Girl's Guide to Negotiating by Leslie Whitaker & Elizabeth Austin (Little, Brown & Company, 2002, ISBN 0316601470, $13.95).

Recommended Web Sites

University of San Francisco's Career Services Center Guide to Negotiating Salary & Benefits:
www.usfca.edu/usf/career/salary.html

Bureau of Labor Statistics—Evaluating a Job Offer:
http://www.bls.gov/oco/oco20046.htm

University of Oklahoma Job Evaluation Matrix—Evaluate and compare job offers:
http://ou.placementmanual.com/jobsearch/jobsearch-04.html

Florida State University's Etiquette Survival Guide:
www.career.fsu.edu/ccis/guides/etiquette.html

The Federal Trade Commission's Credit Scoring:
http://www.ftc.gov/bcp/conline/pubs/credit/scoring.htm

Equifax—Understand and protect your personal credit profile:
http://www.equifax.com

Experian:
http://www.experian.com

TransUnion:
http://www.transunion.com

Backgrounds Online—Sample Background Check Report:
www.backgroundsonline.com/Sample.asp

Yahoo! HotJobs Top Candidate Background Check:
http://hotjobs.choicetrust.com

Conclusion: Making It When You're Midcareer

Congratulations! You've made a huge accomplishment—finding and accepting a new job. You've been brave enough to change your life, and possibly the lives of those close to you, for the better. You may have moved, taken a pay cut, gone back to school, or just changed your commute—regardless, you're making the move toward a great new worklife.

But, of course, there are a few obstacles that midcareer professionals have to confront as they begin a new adventure—especially if they haven't changed jobs in a while. There are some issues you may have to face simply because of where you are in your career and where you will fit in at your new company.

In this chapter we'll examine the unique problems facing midcareer professionals starting a new job—and how to overcome them to make your new job your best yet!

Middle of the Road

Despite your excitement about your new job, there may be some discomfort as you settle in due to your age, experience, or other factors outside your control.

"A major frustration for midcareer professionals has everything to do with that 'mid' prefix," says Joelle, a facilities and events manager for a large university. "At this stage, you're often too young to be afforded maximum respect by some members of senior management, but too old to be considered knowledgeable about current trends by the younger workers. It's almost like dating—with whom can you ally when you're too old for frat parties but too young for the Bingo Hall?"

As you start your new position, you may quite literally find yourself in the "middle" of things, having to prove your authority to those subordinate to you, and trying to prove your experience to those above.

No one likes being the new kid on the block. After garnering a wealth of experience in your illustrious career thus far, you may feel awkward and insecure starting over at a new company. Embrace this opportunity. It's a chance to start from scratch with a new team that doesn't hold the same baggage and expectations (good or bad) as your old colleagues. Carve the niche for yourself that you want. Here are some final tips as you embark on your next big journey.

Practice Patience

When you first started out in the working world, you didn't really have to prove yourself. You were young, perhaps fresh out of college, and while you certainly intended to do a great job, you weren't expected to hit the ground running.

But now you've got more experience behind you. It's assumed that you'll come into the new job knowing your stuff. In fact, you might have been hired specifically to quickly fill a role and produce immediate results.

Accept that you're going to make mistakes. Even the most seasoned worker will face a learning curve at a new job. So be patient, humble, and maintain a sense of humor, and before you know it, new employees will be coming to *you* for answers.

THERE ARE NO DUMB QUESTIONS (REALLY!)

No employee is an island—especially a new one. Seek help early and often:

- ☼ Don't be afraid to ask questions. Better to get answers now than try to look smart and wind up causing bigger problems.

- ☼ Sure you want to prove your value, but don't promise to come up with solutions on your own—work together with the proper people and resources, rather than setting off on a project by yourself.

- ☼ Sign up for on-site training classes, and find a coworker who can help get you up-to-speed on any custom software you haven't used before. Also, read through the employee manual and any other guides to get a good grasp of your new corporate landscape.

- ☼ Attend on- and off-site seminars and conferences, and volunteer for committees, even though you are new. Such assignments will help you learn not only about your new job but about the inner workings and who's who in your company and industry.

If you do the best you can to learn and catch up to everyone else, no one can blame you on the days you struggle.

KEEP YOUR NETWORK

You've worked hard to build your network. Don't let it fall apart now that you are employed again.

You've informed everyone in your network that you've found employment—but continue to seek their help and advice. And be a resource for them as well—when you see a job opening at your new company, pass it along. It's the right thing to do, and you might even score a "referral bonus" cash payout from HR as well.

Most important, you'll need your network as you progress through this job and into others. Look to expand your network at your new job. Mentors, managers, coworkers, friends of managers and coworkers—meet people. Do what you can to add them to your network—and yourself to theirs. It can pay off repeatedly as you follow your career path.

LET YOUR MENTOR BE YOUR GUIDE

As we discussed in chapter 3, a mentor can be a great guide in your job and your career overall. Begin now looking for a person you can trust for help. Some companies have formal mentoring programs; if not, a mentor can be someone within your company—your manager, your manager's manager, or even an employee in a completely different department. Remember, the best mentors are not just people you admire, but those who can help you advance in your career path as well.

ADAPT TO ACHIEVE

In your new job, you may be working at the same level in the same industry; however, in a new company, you may find that things run very differently from what you're accustomed to. The sooner you adapt, the better. Certainly, if you know of a better way to do things, by all means speak up. But resist the temptation to say, "Well, at my *old* job we did it this way..." Be a team player and you may find that this new company's methods actually suit you better.

DON'T MAKE THE SAME MISTAKES

Finally, if you left a previous job because you weren't able to spend enough time with your family, your health was suffering, or you were doing marketing analysis when you actually wanted to do creative writing for marketing campaigns, don't go from the frying pan into the fire. You changed jobs for a reason—keep that reason in the forefront of your mind when you're tempted to agree to work weekends or find yourself picking up the slack for a lagging coworker.

Bon Voyage

We've come to the end of our journey—for now. We hope we've helped you in some way to find a remarkable position that draws on all your strengths and skills, a job you absolutely love with a company where you want to stay forever.

But, as we've said, chances are it won't be long before fantastic, accomplished you is ready for even bigger and better things. And we couldn't ask for anything more!

As you prepare to brave new career waters, we hope the advice we've offered will make you feel more certain about your future, no matter what storms may come your way. And when the waters get rough—or fork in two exciting new directions and you don't know which way to go—we hope you'll let us guide you once again. Good luck!

Recommended Books

Who Moved My Cheese?: An Amazing Way to Deal with Change in Your Work and in Your Life by Spencer Johnson, M.D., & Kenneth Blanchard (Penguin, 1998, ISBN 0399144463, $19.95).

Stop Living Your Job, Start Living Your Life: 85 Simple Strategies to Achieve Work/Life Balance by Andrea Molloy (Ulysses Press, 2005, ISBN 1569754535, $12.95).

Don't Sweat the Small Stuff at Work: Simple Ways to Minimize Stress and Conflict While Bringing Out the Best in Yourself and Others by Richard Carlson (Hyperion, 1998, ISBN 0786883367, $11.95).

The Pathfinder: How to Choose or Change Your Career for a Lifetime of Satisfaction and Success by Nicholas Lore (Simon & Schuster, 1997, ISBN 0684823993, $15.00).

Recommended Web Sites

Yahoo! Health—Work/Life:
http://health.yahoo.com/health/centers/work_life

Professionals in Transition Support Group:
www.jobsearching.org

U.S. Department of the Interior's Online Career Transition Course:
www.doi.gov/octc/strategy.html

INDEX